THE GIFT OF A DAUGHTER

Subhadra Butalia is a veteran activist of the women's movement in India. She was involved in the nationalist movement in the 1940s and later became involved in the women's movement. Subhadra runs Karmika, a legal aid and counselling centre for women victims of domestic violence, dowry abuse etc.

At eighty-one, she is a fond and proud grandmother of four grandchildren.

The Gift of a Daughter

Encounters with Victims of Dowry

SUBHADRA BUTALIA

PENGUIN BOOKS

Penguin Books India (P) Ltd., 11 Community Centre, Panchsheel Park, New Delhi 110 017, India
Penguin Books Ltd., 80 Strand, London WC2R 0RL, UK
Penguin Putnam Inc., 375 Hudson Street, New York, NY 10014, USA
Penguin Books Australia Ltd., 250 Camberwell Road, Camberwell, Victoria 3124, Australia
Penguin Books Canada Ltd., 10 Alcorn Avenue, Suite 300, Toronto, Ontario M4V 3B2, Canada
Penguin Books (NZ) Ltd., Cnr Rosedale & Airborne Roads, Albany, Auckland, New Zealand

First published by Penguin Books India 2002

Copyright © Subhadra Butalia 2002

Typeset in Sabon by Mantra Virtual Services, New Delhi
Printed at Saurabh Print-O-Pack, Noida

For my mother, Dayawanti,
and my father, Dr Parasram,
for teaching me to fight injustice
and
for my husband, Joginder,
in memory of a long and wonderful partnership

Contents

Preface

This small book is neither a memoir nor a book about dowry. A memoir would have had large chunks of my life in it, but these are missing here. A book about dowry would have had much more background information, analysis and history; this has none of these. What then is this book about and why should the reader be interested in it? This is a question I often asked myself while writing. Let me try to answer it here.

I have been working, for many years now, with women who are victims of domestic violence, battery, assault, rape and, principally, dowry. When I began work, I did not expect that much of it would focus on dowry. Over the years I found that we (in Karmika, the group in which I worked) focussed more and more on appeals for legal action or redress by parents of young women who had been cruelly and callously done to death for not having brought enough dowry and requests for help with recovering dowry after a woman had been thrown out of her marital home. We found parents who were in a continual state of crisis because they were unable to meet the recurrent demands for dowry; we had to deal with the desire, on the part of young women, for a dowry, something they could call their own; and much more. As we got deeper into the work we had taken on, I began to realize exactly how widespread dowry was and what an amazing patriarchal consensus there existed on the ground between men of all kinds, from all classes and backgrounds that dowry was their just due and that it was the task of the woman they married to provide them with this. Whether it was husbands, fathers, policemen, lawyers, judges, indeed even lawmakers, politicians or anyone else you cared to name, they all subscribed to this view.

Part of the desire to write this book grew out of this realization, which I wanted to communicate. But there were other things too: I thought it would be useful to share the kinds of experiences we had been through in our group and, as I began to put down case history after case history, I realized how useful the exercise was for me too in attempting to understand the system of dowry. Our work in Karmika grew out of more activist, street-level protest where we attempted to raise awareness about dowry and the devaluation of hundreds of women as a result of the increasing importance given to this. We took out demonstrations, marches and protests of all sorts, and finally put together a street play on dowry. As we took the play from place to place, people came to us with their problems, seeking advice, legal counsel or just an ear to listen to. And we responded to this by setting up Karmika. Thinking we were answering a felt need, we had also naively imagined that we would be able to make a difference. The many years that have passed since Karmika was set up have made me realize the enormity of the task we had set ourselves, and its near impossibility.

For what we have learnt is that it takes more than just a women's group to make a difference. Indeed, we need a gargantuan effort—one that must involve more than just women's groups, more than just women, more than just our social institutions or the state or the judiciary—to address this problem, which every day adds to the violence being perpetrated on women and which is spreading so fast that it is difficult to know how to control it.

It is for this reason that I have put together this book. For the most part it contains a history of one attempt to address the issue of dowry. I have tried to do this by exploring my own growing understanding of the problem, as it manifested itself in my life, and then my thoughts as I saw its much uglier manifestations in the lives of the many women we came across or whose tragic stories we heard. In many ways what you will see in this book are the stories of those women who have faced, and some who have tried to fight, this problem. I do not know if these stories will help to develop an understanding of dowry or of what it is that impels people to demand it and give it. But my attempt to put this book together—inspired, I have to say, by my children urging me to do so as they sat around our dinner table—is born out of a wish, a hope, that this is what this book can begin to do.

Alongside the stories of women caught in the web of dowry, this book tells the story of the struggle of a small women's group to find its feet and to continue to do its work. Our work in Karmika was not at all political—indeed when we began, we told ourselves we would keep away from politics and would not allow ourselves to be caught particularly by party politics—but even so we faced so much harassment and opposition that it makes me wonder how much more the openly political groups would have to face.

Despite this, however, the work has to go on, and just as I have found myself getting depressed and frustrated by the way in which women get caught in this net, sometimes willingly and sometimes through coercion, I have drawn hope from the many young women who have resolved to fight violence in their lives and have grown strong in the process. This book is as much for them as it is for their sisters whose lives dowry has destroyed. If these words that I have penned in the twilight of my life—I am eighty-one years old now and continue to work in Karmika—can help make a difference to their lives, even if it is only minuscule, that will be enough for me.

A Rude Introduction

Dowry was never an important issue in my life. I remember that when we were children, my mother would occasionally worry how she would provide dowry for her six daughters, but my father would always scotch that concern. He was determined not to give dowry. 'I'd rather let my daughters stay single,' he would say. 'I'll give them the very best in education, but I refuse to marry them to anyone who wants dowry.' I have always regretted that he did not live long enough to see that none of his daughters carried dowry with her into her married home.

In my married home though dowry was important. My mother-in-law grumbled constantly that despite having such a handsome and accomplished son, she had not been able to get what he was worth when he married. And when her other sons married and their wives brought dowry, she taunted me, often telling them to show me their dowry to make me jealous. This however was the extent of her dissatisfaction: the occasional bout of anger, some grumbling here and there, none of the violence that has come to be associated with dowry today and that was there even in the past.

At the time however I felt deeply hurt at my mother-in-law's taunts. I had no idea then that dowry would become an obsession with me years later—albeit in a very different way from what one might have expected. I did realize though that it made little difference whether or not you brought dowry: I was at the receiving end for not having brought anything, my sisters-in-law were at the receiving end for not having brought enough. Either way, you lost.

Looking back now I realize that my mother-in-law was very much a product of her time. She was only doing what other women of her generation did—dowry was a part of their culture and often they talked of Ram and Sita and told stories about characters in Hindu mythology who had got dowry. Whenever they went to a wedding they were interested in only two things: what the girl looked like and how much dowry she had brought. In that sense, I suppose I am also a product of my time: I often felt hurt by my mother-in-law's taunts and sometimes I even wept because her barbs were so sharp, but I did not want to complain against her to my husband and I had nowhere else to go. My home had been left behind in Pakistan as a result of Partition, my father was long dead and my mother had been kept back by my younger brother who had stayed on in the family home in Pakistan. My two elder sisters were married and we had never been very close. I had no home other than my married home to call my own, nowhere really to go in times of crisis. So I kept my peace. In the early years of our marriage, I thought these problems were unique to my situation. Today, this is a situation I have come to be familiar with—despite the passage of more than half a century, little seems to have changed in women's lives. More often than not, married women still have nowhere to go and if they do it is not unusual for their families to refuse to take them back.

After Partition, when my husband and I got married, we settled in Ambala. Here, I qualified as a teacher and worked in a college. But the family still remained something of an extended family with my mother-in-law and my husband's younger siblings staying with us (my husband was the eldest in the family and in the absence of his father, who had died in 1948, it was his responsibility to look after the family). It was only in the 1960s when we moved to Delhi that the possibility of change became real. By this time my husband's siblings were more or less settled and my mother-in-law could therefore spend time in their homes as well. But as Delhi was a much more expensive place to live in than Ambala was, I took on a teaching job and although much of my time was spent in balancing work and home and the demands of four young children, as well as learning how to live in a nuclear family rather than in an extended one, I still managed to have some measure of independence. In the 1970s, we were finally able to save some money and buy a small plot of land to build our home. While we were building and for some time before that, we lived in a rented house in a middle-class area of Delhi called Jangpura.

Just across the road from us was a big house into which an extended family of industrialists had recently moved. As their business in electronics—until then quite small—had suddenly begun to grow, they moved from a small, crowded home in a nearby commercial area to this spacious, virtually new middle-class house. The younger son and his wife lived in a room that directly faced the balcony of our house. They had been married for over a year and had a little baby with whom I often saw the young mother playing. Her husband kept long hours at work and she was clearly lonely. This despite the fact that there were three generations of family staying in the house. But clearly, because Hardeep was the daughter-in-law, she was not very popular. We did occasionally see her with her husband and we knew that he was violent towards her for we often heard her crying. I felt her loneliness keenly—in my younger days I too had felt like this—and perhaps she sensed it for, without many words being exchanged, a sort of bond seemed to build up between us.

I will never forget the afternoon Hardeep Kaur was set on fire. I came out on to the small balcony of our house shortly after lunch. Somewhere at the back of my mind I registered smoke coming out of Hardeep Kaur's house. And suddenly, her screams rent the air. The husband and wife often had noisy arguments and confrontations which, as neighbours, we ignored. But this was something different. The girl was burning, she was screaming and people from the houses around rushed out. It was as if we were all paralysed, and we were still standing and staring when a taxi drew up in front of the house and Hardeep was brought out, wrapped in a white sheet. She needed support to make it to the taxi and she was rushed off to hospital. The neighbours who had collected in small groups to talk gradually dispersed and quietly filed back to their homes.

We learnt later that Hardeep had been badly burnt: 70 per cent burns, the doctor said. He didn't hold out much hope, not with burns like that. She might survive a couple of weeks, he said, but no more. Our landlady, who knew the family well, described how Hardeep had been facing a great deal of harassment in the past few months. The previous year her husband's family had even sent her back to her parents with a long list of demands which had to be met before she would be allowed to return. She stayed at her parents' home for six months; then there was a council of the elders of the family and it was decided that she must 'be returned'. The family apologized to Hardeep's husband and his parents for the meagre dowry she had brought, they added more and sent her back. This went on for a while. Sometime later, Hardeep's father died, and her brother did not have enough money to meet the continuing demands of her in-laws. But the question that kept bothering me was: why? Why could her parents not have kept Hardeep? How could they have been so indifferent to her unhappiness? Did she not count for anything? What must *her* feelings have been when she was forced to go back to her husband's home?

The day after this incident I scanned the newspapers. I was surprised to find that none of them had carried the story of Hardeep's burning. I was curious: why? Surely it was just the kind of thing the media loved to write about. When I asked one of my neighbours, he said, why do you bother? It's a matter between the husband and the wife. Perhaps she did something to offend him. But why, I asked, why try to kill her for that? He had no answer. I was amazed at the indifference of the neighbours. They'd been quick to come out to watch the spectacle, but after that they were simply not bothered. In fact, Mrs Tara, who lived next door to us, was reported to have remarked on how 'terrible young girls were these days'. She resolved to send her daughter-in-law to her parents' home so that she would be away from what she called the terrible influence of 'these girls' (presumably she meant Hardeep, who was now virtually at death's door). No matter, I thought, soon the police would start making enquiries and then the neighbours, including me, would have to speak. But a week passed and no one came. I tried to talk to one of my colleagues who happened to be a member of a powerful political party.

I thought perhaps she would be able to suggest something, although I wasn't really clear what it was I wanted to happen. But she had little to add to what the others had said. It's best not to interfere in domestic affairs, she said. I was at a loss about what to do. Today, I would not feel the same bewilderment, but at that time I knew so little and thought the matter ended there.

Then, one afternoon, two women walked into my house. They had come to enquire about the girl across the road, they said. Did I know anything? I was curious: who were these people? And why should I tell them what I knew? They told me they belonged to a women's group, or rather the women's wing of a political party called the Janata Dal, and that they were very concerned about what had happened and wanted to see if there was any way they could help. For the first time after that terrible incident, someone actually wanted to know. I was enormously relieved and told them what I had seen and how disturbed I was that the police had not made any effort to investigate the matter in any depth.

Perhaps it was under pressure from them that the police were forced to carry out the investigation and finally, one day, not too long after the visit of the two women, they came to my house to question me. From them I learnt that Hardeep had given a statement—a dying declaration, for she died within two weeks of the incident—in the presence of a magistrate in which she had exonerated her husband but said she was burnt by her mother-in-law and her grandmother-in-law. On the basis of this statement a charge sheet was filed and the case sent to court. Interestingly, it was only when the police took on the case in earnest that it became news—till then, the violence towards Hardeep and the loss of her life had not mattered. But women's groups began to speak up: a small number of them initially held a meeting behind the house where Hardeep was killed and it was here that I first spoke publicly about Hardeep's death. I told them all I had seen.

Somehow Hardeep's death catalysed something in my memory. I began to remember all sorts of things I had not really noticed before. One of our neighbours in Lahore, it was rumoured, had somehow killed his daughter-in-law in childbirth. Many people talked about this but at the time, when we were young, this story did not even touch me, except that it lodged itself somewhere in my subconscious and came back to haunt me when Hardeep went. And I felt Hardeep's loss keenly—I felt I'd got to know her. Even though we did not talk much, her presence in the room across the road had become a part of my daily life. And now suddenly she was gone, and the place was empty.

The more I tried to get Hardeep out of my system, the more her story clutched at my heart. I decided to write about it and began to collect information. I went to the office of the Mahila Dakshata Samiti, a women's organization, because it was they who had come to see me in the beginning. I learnt from their files that in 1975—the international year of women—some 350 women had been burnt to death in Delhi alone. And this was according to police reports; indeed the police commissioner at the time felt that the number of cases must have been at least twice as many. While many parents of victims protested the deaths of their daughters and complained that they suspected the women had been killed, the police ignored these claims and filed the cases as accidental deaths caused by the 'bursting' of kerosene stoves.

As one of the neighbours who had seen something, I was summoned to court to give evidence in Hardeep's case, as were others from our area. One of my neighbours excused herself on the plea that her eyesight was very weak and she could not therefore be sure of what she had seen and so could not give a statement in court. Everyone knew that she usually did not miss a thing that went on in the street. My landlady said she was not willing to upset the equation she had with her neighbours (that is, Hardeep's husband's family). The biggest shock though was that even Hardeep's brother was unwilling to testify against her marital family—he had apparently been given a large amount of money in exchange for his silence. Hardeep had already become a non-person.

I thought I would talk to her brother. So one morning I went to see him. I told him that the general talk about him was that he had taken a payoff from the husband's family and had agreed to remain silent. Was this true? He was quite straightforward in his reply: whether or not he'd been paid off, he said, was not the issue. Hardeep was gone. What was important for him now was his family, his business and his widowed mother. If he kept chasing the case, all this would fall by the wayside, so he had decided that since Hardeep was dead anyway he would focus on the living.

In trying to understand his indifference, I learnt that in a criminal case the state conducts the prosecution. The aggrieved parties can only depend on the state prosecutor—who is not usually known to be particularly sympathetic. 'Let the state do its prosecution,' Hardeep's brother told me. 'And if the state means business, my sister's death will be avenged and there will be some sort of justice.' Later, much later, I began to realize that he was right. Dowry cases drag on for years and years, and for the families of victims they become an ordeal rather than a search for justice. In many cases relatives of the victims just give up because cases take up so much time. In the lower courts you sit for hours on end and wait and sometimes the magistrate does not turn up or the defence reports sick and the case is adjourned. In one case I learnt about later (that of Parveen Rana) it took two judges six years to determine the nature of a dowry case!

Hardeep's brother was not the only one who was indifferent. I discovered that indifference works at all levels. For example, all those people who had collected in the streets when they heard Hardeep's screams refused to speak up when it came to giving evidence in court. One said, 'After all, we have to live here and we don't want to ruin our relationship with our neighbours.' For most people what had happened was 'just a domestic quarrel', and then there were those who put the blame squarely on Hardeep, claiming, as people often do, that she must have caused trouble by 'talking too openly' with someone or not being meek enough in the home.

It was this hypocrisy that made me decide that, no matter what, I would speak up in court. I made no secret of my decision. A few days before the date of giving evidence, Hardeep's father-in-law visited me. After the initial polite exchanges, he came straight to the point. 'My mother is very old,' he said. 'What is the point of putting her through the harassment of going to court? If you are willing to change your statement, I'll manage the rest and, as a gesture of my gratitude, if you were to come to our shop and choose whatever you want, I'd make you a gift of it.' I was amazed and wondered if this was how silence had been bought from all the others—the neighbours and the relatives. Today, seeing how common such practices are, I know I need not have wondered.

I heard him out though. And I said to him, 'Look, I have no enmity towards you or your family. But I will stick to the truth. I hardly knew the girl. But I cannot lie about what I saw, especially when I am under oath.' He was disappointed and later, when he met my husband, he complained that I 'did not know what I was missing' and he made a veiled threat. My family was worried. My husband warned me that they might attack me while I was out on my morning walk. Indeed, for many days after that incident, he would wait at the door for me to come back in the mornings, and then, gradually, he forgot!

I appeared before the judge and described what I had seen. The defence counsel, a very well-known lawyer, tried to insinuate that I had a hidden motive—perhaps enmity or something towards the family—and that was why I was giving evidence. I stood my ground, however, and answered all questions that were put to me. I think my evidence was largely instrumental in getting the family convicted. However, they immediately filed an appeal with the high court and also deployed another common trick: claiming the mother-in-law and the grandmother-in-law were both very ill, the family had them admitted to hospital. The case dragged on in the high court for a couple of years but finally they were convicted.

A Sense of Injustice

With hindsight I realize that my struggle against dowry did not actually start with Hardeep's death. But that terrible incident brought to the surface a sense of injustice that had actually been impressed upon me principally by my father's ideas on dowry. It catalysed something in my mind. I began to remember different incidents in my life which could have had direct and indirect associations with dowry. Until Partition the offices of the *Tribune*, where my husband then worked, had been in Lahore. After August 1947 they moved first to Shimla and then to Ambala. In Ambala we lived in a large, spacious house and my younger sister came to stay with us. She was young, attractive and very sporty—she enjoyed a game of badminton and tennis. We would often go to our local club in the evenings to play or just to meet others and relax. I noticed that a young armed forces officer seemed very interested in her. He sometimes walked us home and would stay back for a cup of tea. He became quite friendly and one day he even brought along a ball of wool (actually several) asking for a sweater to be knitted—at the time a sign of great intimacy. (Unfortunately, the sweater got eaten up and had to be darned later.)

Being the elder sister, and a sort of replacement parent, I decided to check this man out, to find out what he intended, instead of just letting things drift. One day, I asked him to join us for dinner. I told my sister what I meant to ask him and she was quite excited. We arranged that she would leave the room for a while so that he and I could have a private chat. Accordingly, after a pleasant dinner and a great deal of good conversation, my sister made an excuse and left and I edged my way towards broaching the subject. First we talked about his family, the service conditions under which he had to work and other things. Then I brought the conversation round to my sister and told him of the many obstacles we had had to overcome in order for her to finish her education. 'Yes,' he said, 'now that all that is over you must be quite happy.' I agreed and said I was looking forward to the day when she would be married. 'I find you spending a fair amount of time with her these days,' I said.

'Yes, I like her very much and would like to marry her.'

'I'm happy to know this. She likes you a great deal, and all our relatives know this so they will be happy too to have you in our family. But I must make it very clear that there is no dowry in this marriage.'

He almost fell out of his chair and his face paled, but he put up a brave front. Then he said, almost despite himself, 'But I thought you were one of the richest families of Lahore.' I was a bit taken aback. I had expected some sort of reaction, but nothing so blatant as this. Still, I explained patiently, 'My father was reasonably well off. But he is now dead and gone, and anyway, even had he been alive, he wouldn't have given any dowry. He was totally against it. He thought marriages should be partnerships of love and friendship, not bargaining counters for money.' The young officer smiled and said weakly that he agreed and added that my sister was very beautiful and beauty itself was a sort of dowry. I was happy; I thought even if he did not believe strongly in what he was saying, he had at least made a beginning in doing so and I looked forward to having him as my brother-in-law. He was to come back the next day so that we could finalize things. We never saw him again.

My sister was deeply unhappy, and part of the unhappiness was directed at me. I was unhappy too—and somewhat confused. I felt a terrible sense of guilt. Had I done the right thing? Could I not have scraped together a sort of dowry? Did I have the right to impose my views on my sister, especially when they affected her life? I had no answers to these questions and I battled with them on my own, without anyone to discuss them with. Eventually, things took their own course. My sister married someone who was totally against dowry, so we did not have to worry on that count. Today, when I look back on that incident I sometimes wonder: if I had agreed to that marriage, would my sister too have joined the long line of nameless women who count as 'dowry deaths'? This thought fills me with dread for something that could have been so likely.

But if one sister's potential marriage fell through because of a lack of dowry, another—my elder sister— had a different story to tell. She had married a man she loved and the way their relationship developed is a story in itself. It began on a bus ride. While we were still in school, the two of us had gone to visit a friend in Model Town. On the way back I wanted to walk home—we lived very close by—but my sister insisted on taking a bus. So we went our separate ways: she by bus and I on foot. In the bus there was a young, good-looking army officer and, as he told us later, he took one look at her and fell in love instantly. Since Model Town was a small place at the time, it wasn't difficult for him to trace her to our family home. He did what men who were thus smitten often did at the time: he wrote her a long love letter.

The letter was received and opened by my father, again something that wasn't unusual in that day and age. He showed it to my mother and her sister, who were with him at the time, and my masi lost no time in bringing the information to us, though she wasn't very clear about who the love letter was written to, which was really frustrating. My father did not discuss it with any of us, of course, but he wrote back to the young man telling him that his daughter was too young to marry—she was still in school—and that when a young man seeks a young woman's hand in marriage, it is the parent who should be approached. Writing letters directly to the young woman was not the done thing. The young officer immediately sent a letter of apology and said, in what I thought was a cowardly fashion, that he had written to my sister purely 'as a brother' because he did not have a sister to call his own. My father laughed when he read the letter, called the man a coward and forgot about the whole incident.

My father died soon after this. My mother was left with six unmarried girls in the house—something that was seen as a major problem. It was at this time that a cousin of ours suggested that we try to locate the young man who had declared his love for my sister and see if he was still interested. We did and he was. He came and negotiations began again. He told us he was very much in love with her, but that he would like an early marriage because he had to join duty soon and would like to marry before that. There was a lot of excitement in the family because this was the first happy occasion after my father's death, which had devastated us all. We all got down to shopping for the bride, buying clothes, things for the house and everything that we could get hold of.

The day of the wedding arrived. We had expected the bridegroom to bring a large party of guests and were very surprised—and also a little bit disappointed—when just a handful of people arrived. They came quietly, with no music or noise, walked in and sat down to eat. After they had eaten, the marriage ceremony took place and the bridegroom took the bride away. But he left behind all the dowry we had purchased with such excitement. We were terribly disappointed at the time but now I think of my brother-in-law with great respect. The marriage took place in 1937 and for a man to have such conviction at the time must have been rare. Throughout his life, my brother-in-law always spoke proudly of how he had spent only fifty rupees on his marriage.

But my brother-in-law was a rare man. My own brother, who was just a child at the time, was quite different. For much of his life, he lived in my home and I put him through school and university. Then we found a suitable match for him and the engagement was finalized. To my surprise, sometime after this he came to me saying he had brought a fresh proposal and when I asked him why, he gave dowry as the reason. Because all this was so much a part of the life we lived at the time, I did not think anything of it, though I did not let him marry the second person he suggested. But now, when I look back on it, I realize that my sense of injustice about dowry and what it does to women must have been formed from the accumulated weight of these experiences.

Both before and after I got married I had to shoulder a lot of family responsibilities. When my father died, I was left with the responsibility of looking after my younger siblings. My sisters were soon married and my mother did not keep well, so there was no one other than I to take on the care of the others. Later, shortly after I was married, my father-in-law died and I then took on the care and upbringing of my brother-in-law as well. My sister-in-law (my husband's younger sister) lived in a hostel and came home only at weekends and during the holidays. She was the youngest in her family—there were five brothers before her—and everyone wanted her to make a good match. Negotiations were on with various families and when things went well in terms of mutual understanding with one of them, we decided it was time to have a meeting of both 'clans' to sort things out.

One evening we received a telegram from the prospective groom's mother saying she would be reaching Ambala (where we lived) by the first train the next morning. We spent the whole night cleaning and scrubbing our home, which was usually in a state of chaos, excited at the prospect of this visit, nervous that she might find a speck of dirt here or there. We had barely finished when, at six in the morning, she arrived. 'I'm famished,' she said as we met her at the station, 'is your home far from the station? Can we stop on the way for a cup of tea and something to eat?' Our home was barely five minutes away so we took her home and gave her breakfast. She was critical of both the quantity and the kind of food we gave her and privately I thought her quite arrogant, but then I told myself she had come to visit us to approve a bride for her son and I should behave like elder sisters-in-law were expected to in such a situation. This virtually meant letting her get away with anything. After breakfast she wanted hot water for a bath, but before that she announced she had decided to wash her hair and she wanted Gudia (which is the affectionate term we used for my young sister-in-law) to oil her hair. Gudia was duly summoned to perform this duty, which she did meekly. I was surprised to see this aspect of hers—she was usually quite self-willed, yet here she was behaving like a coy and docile little thing. This, I thought, is what the prospect of marriage does to a woman.

I was deeply unhappy at the prospect of this proposed match. I did not like the woman who was visiting us. She behaved as if she owned the house and all of us were there simply to do her every bidding. When it was time for her to leave, she demanded that we make some aloo parantha and pack them for her to carry on the train. She didn't want to eat them on the train. 'I don't have anyone to cook for me, so this will help when I reach home,' she said. 'And don't forget to put in that bottle of pickle that I liked so much. You can make another one for yourself.' This left me open-mouthed, since we had no one to cook for us either, and most of the time the task fell on me.

My unhappiness was not however shared by my mother-in-law. According to her the prospective bridegroom's mother could do what she wanted, and we, as the bride's family, had to accommodate her every wish and desire. 'But don't you realize that between them she and her son will make your daughter's life miserable and they'll constantly pester us with their demands?' I asked. But she saw nothing out of the ordinary in that. I found I was in a one-person minority in my protest and discomfort. The brothers said, 'After all, she is our sister and why should we not give her everything we can? If they ask, let them; we're happy to give.'

Nor were they particularly upset by the behaviour of the prospective mother-in-law. Rather, they were happy that she was forthright, particularly in her demands. They said, 'We've only one sister and God has given us enough to meet any dowry demands there are for her. This is our duty.' When I tried to protest, my mother-in-law put me in my place by saying I had no business to protest or interfere in a problem that had nothing to do with me. No matter that it was taking place in my house, but that, according to all of them, was a secondary thing. So there was nothing to do but wait for the expected proposal of marriage to come. Today I know—and in some ways I knew even then— that such events are common in our lives and families. Indeed, in some ways they are almost procedural. First the prospective in-laws 'see' the young woman, and if they approve she (or her photograph) is 'shown' to the man in question, and it is only if he approves that further proceedings take place. But for us, this next step turned out to be a bit of a bombshell.

A few days after her visit, the mother-in-law-to-be wrote a sort of letter of thanks to say how much she had enjoyed our hospitality and that she had written to her son saying she had found a charming bride for him. She said he was looking forward to meeting her. He had asked for time off from his employers to come and meet the prospective bride. And then she suggested that we send the man a ticket to pay for his travel. And this was not all: she thought it would be a good idea for the two young people to get to know each other and suggested that we not only invite him over but pay for the two of them to go away somewhere for a few days together.

For me—for us generally, I think—this was the last straw. I don't know if she was testing our tolerance or if she really meant what she said. Even my mother-in-law was angry. 'What does this woman take us to be?' she shouted. 'Send my daughter alone to Shimla with a stranger?' So the negotiations were called off. Later my mother-in-law took her daughter away from me because she was not happy with my views on dowry and thought I might influence her young daughter. I was sad to lose her and she too was not happy to go away. She'd had a rough time in life. She was fourteen when her father died and since then she had more or less lived with me. I'd become very fond of her. But I reasoned with myself that her mother did have the right to decide and she had decided to take her away. I had to respect that decision. Many years later she was married in proper style as the only sister of five brothers. I sang and danced the night away at her wedding though I did not share the excitement of examining her dowry as it was being loaded into lorries to be taken away.

The Beginnings of Activism

After Hardeep's death I began to notice that there were on average two dowry cases, sometimes cases of dowry deaths, in the newspapers every day. Looking back now I sometimes think that if Hardeep's case had been an isolated incident, I might have got over it. Perhaps with the passage of time the trauma of what I had seen would have receded. But that did not happen because every morning the newspaper screamed: 'Another dowry death'. As a result the trauma turned into anger. At some stage, those of us who were getting more and more worked up about these incidents began to think we could not just sit around feeling angry. We had to try and intervene in some way. Earlier, some of us had got together and formed a women's group called Stree Sangharsh and after some discussion we decided to take up work on dowry within the group. By this time there were any number of cases we had heard of: Kanchan Chopra, Tarvinder Kaur, Neelam, Shakuntala Arora, Bharati Narula and many others. As a first step we decided to organize a demonstration to protest the death of Tarvinder Kaur.

Tarvinder Kaur had died four months after her marriage, in her husband's home in north Delhi. We later learnt that she and Hardeep had been friends and we were devastated at the deaths of these two young women. Stree Sangharsh mobilized people all over Delhi to protest these and other deaths. We focussed on Model Town, where Tarvinder had lived. We prepared leaflets and posters to tell people about the increasing numbers of dowry deaths in the city and distributed them from house to house. Elsewhere we mobilized people in schools and colleges, among other groups, to participate in the march.

On the appointed day, we assembled in front of Model Town market and marched through the residential area shouting anti-dowry slogans and distributing our leaflets. We were joined by many local people so that by the time we reached our destination—the home of Tarvinder's in-laws—our numbers had swelled considerably. It was a hot summer day, but we hardly felt the heat in our enthusiasm, and several of the neighbours who could not join the march came out of their homes with cold water, soft drinks and food for us. At the house, we pulled out buckets and paintbrushes we had carried with us and painted the perimeter wall black, writing anti-dowry slogans on the black so they would stand out. Tarvinder's in-laws did not dare show their faces outside, so they remained cowering inside the house like mice. We were pleased to see how much support we got among the local residents and after several hours of marching and shouting, we returned to our homes, happy and exhausted. The next day the newspapers were full of our march and we felt we had made a good beginning in drawing attention to the issue of dowry and how widespread it had become. The reports were extremely sympathetic—something that encouraged us greatly. Little did we know then that it takes more than a few demonstrations and newspaper reports to change things that are so ingrained.

Nonetheless, it was the newspaper report that led Satyarani Chadda to our home. She read about the march in the newspapers and went to the locality where Tarvinder had lived. She asked around and was given an address in Jangpura, ours, and she made her way to our home. She was crying when she came to talk. 'They killed my daughter,' she said. 'Shashibala was six months pregnant.'

She described what had happened. One day her son-in-law came to visit her. Her son had just bought a new scooter which he showed his brother-in-law. 'He [her son-in-law] immediately demanded that the scooter be given to him.' When Satyarani told him that it belonged to her son, the son-in-law said he too was her son and she should give it to him. Satyarani said she had in fact booked a scooter for him, but was waiting till his wife— her daughter—had given birth to a son. The son-in-law left in a huff, and the very next day her daughter was burnt to death. Satyarani learnt of this around midnight and rushed to her daughter's home. 'I saw a bundle lying on the floor. This is your daughter, he said. I was horror-struck. I screamed and cursed. They simply stood there. Here, look at these pictures. They told me she got burnt in the kitchen. But she was lying in the courtyard. Here, look.' I did. The small kitchen showed clean walls—no sign of smoke. Surely if someone had been burnt there, the walls would have shown some evidence of it?

But, this apart, what was much more disturbing was Satyarani's own attitude. Understandably, she was inconsolable at her daughter's death. But all the while she wept, she kept saying, 'If only I had waited, if only . . .'

'Waited for what?' I asked, mystified.

'For Shashibala's child to be born,' she said. 'After all, I had already booked a scooter in his name, and if Shashi had given birth to a son, I would have given it to him.'

'But what if it had been a daughter?' I asked in utter disbelief.

'Then I would have waited,' she said innocently.

I was amazed. The grief-stricken mother could see no inconsistency in what she was saying. She wept because she had lost her daughter, but she seemed to see nothing wrong in the system of which her daughter had become a victim.

Satyarani's tragedy became a part of my concern and I began to visit her home regularly to help in her fight for justice. It was during the course of these visits that I became familiar with other members of her family. I noticed that she had two sons and there was a little girl who was often to be found playing in the house. I wondered whose daughter she was and where her mother was. I learnt that she was the elder son's child and that his wife did not live there. I tried to find out why. Satya was evasive, but finally she told me it was because her daughter-in-law insisted not only on working in an office but also on keeping control of her salary—and in an extended family, that was not the norm. The salary, Satya felt, should have been handed over to her. Once again I was struck by the anomalies here: Satya was a victim of the same system which she herself helped perpetuate, but she saw no contradiction in what she felt for her daughter and how she related to her daughter-in-law.

But I realized too that it wasn't right to blame her. She was, after all, a product of her own time and culture. Some years later, when she got her younger daughter married, she did so with considerable fanfare and also gave her a dowry. Fortunately, the marriage worked and her daughter was happy. But her case dragged on for years as Satya ran from pillar to post trying to get some sort of justice on behalf of Shashibala. At one stage we thought it might help to approach the police commissioner. We wrote to him, with a list of ten questions we had drawn up to which we demanded an answer. Needless to say, he did not even bother to acknowledge the letter. I sent a reminder. It met with the same fate. I realized that while the police may be quick to send letters, they see no obligation to respond to those they receive.

Satyarani's daughter's case was the first one we took up. It got a lot of publicity because at that time the issue of dowry and dowry deaths was quite new. As often happens, the media loved the story of a mother fighting for justice for her dead daughter and Satya's home became a regular place for visitors, with both the Indian and the foreign media (for whom dowry deaths were the latest sensation in India) featuring her case and interviews with her. It was this in some ways that turned Satya into a public figure. Though her sorrow weighed heavily on her heart, she was always hospitable and always willing to talk to visitors and media people. It was this too that in some ways set her on the path she was later to take. I admired Satya for her tenacity and persistence but I was also somewhat concerned at what the publicity seemed to be doing to her. But then, I told myself, that was not my concern.

One day, I expressed these concerns to a friend, Viji Srinivasan, who worked at the time at the Ford Foundation. It turned out that she too, as also several others, had been thinking along the same lines. Viji had a wonderful solution to offer: 'I think we should start a short-stay home for women and ask if she'd like to take charge of it.' I was both surprised and pleased to hear of this idea—it seemed that Viji had already anticipated my concern and come up with a solution. Later, with help from Viji and many other women activists, Shakti Shalini, a short-stay home for women in distress, was created, and Satya and another woman, Shah Jahan Apa, who had also lost her daughter to dowry, took charge. They have both been there since then and have run it in their own inimitable style.

Unfortunately the law has not been with Satya in her fight for justice for her daughter. She has knocked on more doors than I can think of, consulted any number of lawyers, and more than eighteen years have gone by but justice remains elusive. This is not only because the system of justice is flawed but also because the profession of law is so full of corruption and indifference. In the early days, many lawyers were ready to jump into the fray and advise and help Satyarani. But after the publicity they hoped to get wore off they couldn't be bothered and often would not even see her. She spent hours waiting in the homes of some of our well-known lawyers, sometimes waiting for 'madam' or 'sir' to wake up, without even being offered a chair or a glass of water. Because she was desperate for justice, Satya bore this humiliation, but for me this was the beginning of my disillusionment with the practitioners of law and justice.

As I began to hear about more and more cases, I realized that these were not isolated incidents. There was a pattern to them, a sort of continuity. Much of the time parents were desperate to marry off their daughters and did not bother to check up on their prospective sons-in-law. For young girls marriage was the be-all and end-all of their lives. And men—or families—found different ways to kill women. This is what happened to Rama Mohanty, an MA from Delhi University. One day her brother in Delhi received a telephone call that Rama was missing from home. He went to Saharanpur, where Rama lived with her husband, to find that she was indeed missing. He filed a report with the police. The next morning the police found a gunny bag with a body stuffed in it, lying in a train compartment quite a distance away from Saharanpur. The body, which had been there for some time, was later identified as Rama's—by her mother and brother who recognized the bangles on the wrist of the dead person.

Rama had been married into a family of moneylenders. Apparently, one daughter-in-law had already died under mysterious circumstances in their house, but Rama's parents, like many others, had been so keen to marry off their daughter that they had ignored all warnings and so married Rama into this family. It was later revealed by the police that Rama had been strangled by her husband and father-in-law, then put in a bag and placed in a train which was en route to Amritsar. The train made the full journey there and back before some passengers noticed the gunny bag, for by then it had begun to smell. They reported this to the police. Meanwhile, Rama's husband was writing false ransom notes to himself and typing them on his own typewriter. He also hid Rama's jewellery and told the police that she had run away with it. All this came to light when he was caught and his house was searched.

The father and son were brought to Delhi because Rama's brother had filed a case there. I remember that we shouted slogans as the men were being marched into the court—some of us were so angry that we even tried to hit out at the men, but we were stopped from doing this by the police, though we did manage to land a couple of blows, which gave us an immense sense of satisfaction! Both men were convicted by the UP High Court (because the crime was committed in UP) but it is not clear whether they managed to get a reversal from the Supreme Court. This happens often in the court procedure. At first there are endless adjournments so that the case drags on and then, if it makes it to its conclusion in the trial court, it moves on to the high court and sometimes even the Supreme Court—something which is, in theory, a positive thing, but which works against the interests of the woman in such cases. During the course of its journey from the trial court to the Supreme Court a case may be handled by various luminaries of the judicial system, not all of whom think alike, although most of them are alike in being almost totally insensitive to women's problems. And then, often in cases where the accused are given bail, they manage to buy off the witnesses or intimidate them into silence. Women's organizations have repeatedly demanded that dowry murders should be made a non-bailable offence but this demand has been met with indifference.

But if Rama's parents were guilty of not having checked out the man they married their daughter to, they were not alone in this. Over the years this problem came up again and again, with parents realizing after they had lost their daughters how willingly they had accepted the man's credentials, which were often totally false. Karuna Jhanji's case demonstrates the full tragedy of such a situation. It was only after she died of burning that Karuna's parents spoke about her husband's past. In their complaint to the police, they pointed out that the husband, Swaran Kumar, had married and divorced his first wife for dowry, that he was known to have been violent to her, that the neighbours had heard him being violent to Karuna and that he had been arrested several years before he married Karuna and was in fact out on bail. In addition, he had several criminal cases filed against him. It seemed he had also bribed the police to tamper with evidence in Karuna's case and had tried to do so at the hospital as well, though this latter was not possible because of an alert and honest doctor. Moreover, he had tried to run away from India to escape conviction despite being banned from leaving the country by the courts. Such a bar is still in force.

Karuna died because her parents were unable to fulfil

her husband's repeated demands for more and more dowry. After her death, her parents sent Karmika a long list detailing the evil deeds of their son-in-law but it was already too late. Her marriage had been unhappy right from the start. At one stage Karuna's father had called in members of the community and his extended family, and through their good offices, a sort of truce was effected. No one questioned why a truce was so necessary when the key problem was the continuing demand for dowry. In their attempt to get justice, Karuna's parents wrote a letter to the then police commissioner. This letter, which is reproduced below, shows tellingly how Karuna had nowhere to go, no one to turn to and how her pleas for help were met with the usual advice to 'go back and adjust'.

Dear Sir

My daughter Karuna Khosla of B 250 Greater Kailash died of serious burns in her husband's house and my husband has already filed an FIR about this at the Greater Kailash Police Station on 14.3.1980. Four years back I married my daughter, Karuna Khosla to Shri Swaran Kumar Khosla on 4.2.1976. But it is my misfortune that my daughter did not have a single day's happiness in her husband's home. My daughter's in-laws, husband, mother-in-law and her sister-in-law who deserted her husband and has been living in her mother's house for the last six or seven years, all used to beat and harass my daughter over the issue of dowry. Parents of course always give to their daughters and accordingly I always gave to my daughter whatever I could. But these dowry wolfs did not appreciate anything. Whenever my daughter expressed a desire to have a new dress made, her mother-in-law always said, 'According to our custom a young bride gets her clothes from her parents' home for the first three years of her marriage.' I fail to understand how a husband could be so indifferent to such desires of his wife. I gave to my daughter four tolas of gold jewellery, but I never saw my daughter wearing any gold whenever she came to visit us. And if ever I asked her she evaded my question, saying that the jewellery is in the locker and it takes time to take it out. Many times my daughter got desperate and came back home to us and then her husband begged and pleaded and gave repeated assurances that she would not have any complaint. He sought forgiveness. This was repeated every time my daughter came home to us after being harassed. One evening, after his return from office he beat her so much that she ran out of the house to save her life and went to the house of a friend of ours, Prakash Aneja, who lived in Hauz Khas. She did not even have two rupees which at that time was the scooter fare which was also paid by Aneja. From there my daughter phoned us and we rushed to Delhi. We picked up our daughter from Aneja's house and went straight to the house of Khosla. When we reached there, we found that already some of his relatives had assembled there. My daughter told them all that she was suffering at the hands of her husband. Khosla's relatives reprimanded him and he apologized. He requested us not to take her away and assured us that in future he would not ill treat her. When my daughter had run to the neighbour's house to escape the beating, Khosla had informed the police that his wife had run away from home.

When my daughter was burnt, he managed to get a statement from her that she was making tea and was burnt because of the gas. But when her neighbours met us in the hospital they told us that when they went to her house they saw that kerosene oil was splattered all over. My daughter was burnt at 9.30 in the morning but she was admitted to hospital only at 11.45. What was happening during these two hours, especially when Safdarjang Hospital is only 20 minutes away from Greater Kailash? And unbelievably, my daughter was 100 per cent burnt.

I hope you will accept the appeal of an unfortunate mother like me and have such a thorough enquiry into this case that such dowry-hungry beasts get the strictest possible punishment. This appeal is accompanied by another copy which has been sent to the Hon'ble President and also to the Prime Minister.

As a sister, I request you to understand my sorrow and order an enquiry into this case as early as possible.

Signed: deceased daughter's mother, Nirmala Jhanji, 18/105 Neelkanth Road, Agra

While Karuna's mother wrote letters, it was her father who had filed the first information report (FIR) with the police when he learnt of Karuna's death. Both the letter and the FIR showed how unhappy Karuna had been and how little attention her parents had paid to her pleas. Here is the text of the FIR.

True copy of cyclostyled letter
First wife divorced and burnt alive
Dowry victim Karuna Khosla case
(FIR no 392/80 Kalka ji police station)
State vs. Swaran Kumar Khosla

The crime: When the new Congress (I) took over there was an overall expectation that crime in Delhi would come down and at least crimes against women and dowry bride burning would be eliminated. But alas! The most heinous dowry burning case perpetrated by an almost crime history-sheeter is being hushed up and the accused, Swaran Kumar, is being shielded.

The crime: When Karuna was married to the dowry-hungry Swaran Kumar in 1976, little did the innocent girl or her father know that she was being sacrificed at the altar of a divorced girl Vinod Bala of Jullundur. He had married Vinod Bala, daughter of Shri Kayshap, and after extracting dowry of [many] lakhs, divorced her. He married Karuna in 1976, she was persecuted, taunted, tortured, physically beaten daily for not bringing sufficient dowry and about six months back turned out of the house by Swaran Kumar. After turning [her] out he overreacted and filed a report . . . at police post Greater Kailash saying his wife had run away. Shri Mohan Lal Jhanji, [Karuna's father] who had tried to make Shri Khosla see reason and abstain from torturing Karuna, collected members of the *biradri* people and Swaran Kumar realising that the opinion of the *biradri* was absolutely against his evil actions, promised to not ill treat her and he took her back. Alas, Karuna had realised that there was a death trap being laid by her husband. From then on the torture intensified, in which Swaran Kumar's brother Mela Ram, mother, younger brother were also equal partners. The said drama culminated on 12.3.1980 when she was burnt alive. In the process of burning her, Swaran Kumar sustained slight burns on his hands. These burns, consistent with his criminal character expertise in cheating, he stated to have incurred in saving her. Is fire such a chooser that it causes only small burns on the hands of the one trying to save victims? Can a burning person remain static so that only the hands of the saviour get some small burns? Ordinary human intelligence says that a person in angry flames would be writhing in panic and throwing his hands, feet and body [about] in which process flames should touch all parts of the body of the saviour. But the police refused to use even this much common sense.

Karuna was burnt at 9.30 a.m. on 12.3.1980 but

not rushed to hospital for over two hours. What was the motive for the delay? Shri Swaran Kumar and his brothers were making preparations to purchase the police and to create influence at the hospital. They were also waiting for her to die so that the need for taking her to the hospital did not arise. When she did not die at home and when Mela Ram and his brother attempted to hush up the crime, she was taken to Safdarjang Hospital. The parents of the girl were intentionally not informed of the crime. They were informed after Swaran Kumar was able to get Karuna's signature on a statement which acquitted him and his brother Mela Ram of all the crime.

Parents of Karuna arrive

Shri Mohan Lal Jhanji, father and Raman Kumar Jhanji, brother of Karuna, reached Delhi and tore their hair and beat their breasts on reaching the hospital and seeing their charred daughter and knowing that the husband after committing the most gruesome crime, had managed to get Karuna's signature on a cooked up statement . . . It is understood that the sister of Swaran Kumar working in Jansanghi school at Paharganj played a prominent part in getting the sympathies of the Metropolitan Council and influencing lower level police.

In any case, in the light of the past history of the man, in view of the devious part played by the local police in this case, it is necessary that the accused is arrested and the agency is entrusted immediately to probe into the crime. Either this case should be referred to the Crime Branch or the CBI to know the real facts so that the dowry-hungry persons get a lesson and hundreds of Karunas are saved from such atrocities. It is again requested that Shri Swaran Khosla may be arrested as early as possible.

The relevant points regarding Karuna's murder are:
1. Why did he not inform his in-laws in time?
2. Why did he not allow the police to take the statement of Karuna in front of her father?
3. S.K. Khosla, an employee of the Food Corporation of India used to leave for his office at 9 a.m. to be in time but on that unfortunate day what was he doing till 9.30 a.m. at his home at G 250 Greater Kailash, New Delhi?
4. Karuna was admitted in the hospital at 11.45 a.m. What happened in the interval between the alleged incident and the admission into the hospital of the deceased, Karuna Khosla?
5. Where are her clothes?
6. What part did local police pay in hushing up the case when it was on the record of the area chowki of Greater Kailash that this person has been filing false reports of elopement etc., against his wife?

Yours faithfully
Mohan Lal Jhanji (unfortunate father)
ML Jhanji
18/105 Neelkanth, City Station Road, Agra, UP.
Dt 16.4.80

No matter how hard Karuna's desperate parents tried to get some semblance of justice, they were faced with obstacles at every step. Slowly it became clear to them that the whole system was against them. The most important thing however was that part of the blame attached to them as well: had they not been in such a hurry to marry off their daughter, had they spent some time researching the man's background, they might have been able to save her life. But the pressure to marry daughters off is difficult to resist. Not only does this pressure come from society but our religious books too add their bit. Of the ten sacraments for salvation, for example, Hindu women are allowed only one: marriage. It is only through marriage and services to the husband that a woman can achieve salvation. An unmarried girl is a burden to her father and if a father does not get his daughter married before she reaches puberty, he is guilty of not performing his duty. And if a girl dies unmarried, it is said she becomes a ghost, whereas for a married woman the fate that awaits her is that of a sumangali (blessed). With the kind of social sanction certain religious and cultural practices have acquired in our society, parents are under considerable pressure to marry off their daughters as early as possible. To do this they offer various attractions to the prospective in-laws. It is this desperation to marry their daughters off that makes parents indifferent or reluctant to check up on their prospective sons-in-law. The marriage becomes more important than the future of the daughter, no matter that the marriage may end up just being a sham.

I remember a young woman called Rekha who had come to us. She told us that her marriage had been fixed in just two hours. She had gone with her parents to another wedding, and there they met a young man who looked very impressive and more or less on the spot her parents decided that this was the man for Rekha. It did not take much time for other things to be decided and before she knew it Rekha found herself married to the man. The marriage lasted longer than it took to be finalized, but that is about all that can be said about it. 'There was nothing to recommend him other than his looks,' said Rekha. 'But I guess that was my fate. In the early days when things were being sorted out, I tried to talk to my parents just to say that this sense of urgency about my marriage did not make sense and filled me at least with a sense of foreboding, but they did not listen to me. I was full of apprehension, but I couldn't say much because we were not supposed to speak in such matters.'

Taking the Message to the Streets

I've spoken earlier of our group Stree Sangharsh. If I am asked today how Stree Sangharsh came together and how we got so deeply involved in the fight against dowry, I would find it difficult to pinpoint a reason and a time. What I do remember is that we were all appalled at the number of deaths that were taking place and we felt we had to do something. But even as we went about the work, our group was going through many upheavals and changes. All of us had come together in the somewhat naive—we know this now, but it was difficult to see this then—belief that we could solve the problems of other women. We never actually stopped to think whether there were any problems of our own that we needed to address. And of course they kept cropping up in the group: there were problems to do with our different ideologies. Our group was made up of women of all ages—some of the younger women had come to women's activism through their involvement with the left movement; others had only the history of activism during the heady days of the nationalist movement as a background; still others had no political involvement at all, but they had a very strong sense of justice. Every decision had to be preceded by long discussions, many cups of tea and much angst, and we tried hard to make decisions collective and to do away with hierarchies. But of course that is easier said than done, and often the fact that one or the other of us might have our picture in the papers became a cause for discussion and ill feeling in the group. Nonetheless, we worked hard and we were full of enthusiasm; we did not need much to pick up our placards and take off for a demonstration or a march. And even though we debated and discussed our differences and our different understandings, this did not come in the way of our work. For myself, I sometimes felt out of place because I was so much older than the others, and often I think this meant that they did not know how to deal with me. Ought they to see me as my daughter's mother (my daughter was also in the group) or as myself? Some of them were actually my daughter's friends and had been in and out of our home—they found it very difficult to relate to me as an equal, yet equality was one of the things we all held dear.

The group had been loosely forming over a period of time, and the women in it had been meeting informally to talk about the kinds of issues they wanted to address. At some point we thought it important to give the group an identity and name, and someone suggested Stree Sangharsh. At the time, we were all fairly sceptical about the kinds of things that we would value today: documenting the birth of such an initiative, keeping a record of how things happened, what sorts of discussions took place and so on. Now I know that such documentation is an essential part of the making of history. But at that stage we met and talked, and sometimes we kept notes and at other times not, with the result that now, when we try to recreate the history of what was without doubt one of the key groups in the movement today, we have nothing to go by but our memories. What I record here then is my memory of that time and of how we came together. Someone else's may well be different.

How did we get involved in dowry work? I'm not really sure. What I do remember is that we had been reading reports of such deaths in the newspapers and it took a while to sink in that this was something that had not happened before—or perhaps we had just not noticed it. But now it was impossible to ignore: every other day the papers carried the news of a young woman dying of burns. Always the excuse was that her clothes had caught fire while she was cooking, that the 'stove had burst'. But how was it that these stoves had suddenly started to burst—we had all been using kerosene stoves for years. And how was it that accidents happened only to young, newly married women? I was particularly keen to work on dowry but others in the group were not as enthusiastic. Several of them felt the issue was basically a cultural one, and they weren't sure they wanted to address it. Today we would be less dismissive of issues we define as 'mere cultural issues' but at that time we had not lived through so many years of religion-based politics. However, even though several of our members saw dowry as a cultural issue, for me it was the main issue I wanted to take up, and I kept on pushing the group to join in doing so. Their initial reluctance gave way to a cautious agreement to take on work on dowry when we started to see more and more reports of cases in the newspapers, and so we got wholly involved in the anti-dowry agitation. This also helped to give the group some sense of direction and stability. From now on, many of our meetings were devoted to discussing dowry and dowry deaths.

Very soon, we worked out a three-pronged strategy. We decided to lobby with the government and demand changes in the existing legislation on dowry, to raise public awareness about the provisions that did exist in the law and to launch an agitation against dowry and dowry deaths and demand that the offenders be given the strictest possible punishment. As always, demonstrations took precedence and this was how we took up the case of Tarvinder Kaur.

As we were planning the demonstration and drafting the leaflets and pamphlets we would distribute to the public, the issue of whose address we should place on the pamphlets came up. We were an informal sort of group and met at different people's houses each time, so we really had no fixed address. This was our first public action and we needed to have an address, so finally, after much discussion, we put down my home address.

Little did I realize the sort of trouble this would lead to. To begin with, none of us anticipated that the demonstration against Tarvinder Kaur's death would get such an amazing response or that it would get so much media attention. While this was wonderful for our campaign, the complication it caused was that newspapers and magazines, given as they are to always identifying things with a particular person or place, used my name quite centrally. And this did not happen only in India. I remember that a British newspaper, *The Observer*, carried a detailed write-up which gave all the credit to me. I did not know the writer at all and had never met him or spoken to him, but in the way that media people are often dishonest, the article gave the impression that he had had a long discussion with me.

When we met the following week to discuss and evaluate the first steps of our campaign, there was hell to pay. My colleagues in the group naturally felt incensed that all the 'glory' had been grabbed by me, and that I was personalizing what was essentially a collective campaign and they complained vociferously. I had a lot of explaining to do but I could not really convince anyone that this was a mistake and there had been nothing malafide or deliberate in this. At first I thought we would get over it—after all, some of us did know each other and we had come together in an atmosphere of trust. But gradually I began to feel it was no use trying to work together if every meeting was spent in argument and explanation. How were we going to solve the problems of other women if we could not address our own? And this was not the only point of disagreement. Other matters also gave us cause to differ in fundamental ways. Some of us were keen that the group have a structure and that we register it so that it would get some credibility. But others were totally opposed to a structure because they felt it would imply a hierarchy (if, say, we had a president or director) and equally opposed to registration or anything resembling it because that would amount to cooperating/colluding with the state. The dominant feeling was that we should function as a collective and not have a hierarchy. As an ideal, this was wonderful but when it came to taking decisions and responsibility, it posed very many practical problems.

But there were things we did together, and which we made a success of. Indeed, it would not be wrong to say that at the time Stree Sangharsh was one of the groups that was in the forefront of the struggle against dowry and rape. Despite the fact that we argued and fought internally, for quite a while we held together as a group and worked on different issues with an enthusiasm and commitment which would be rare to find today. We would get together to protest this or that death, lobby with government, picket police stations and court arrest.

It did not matter if it was night or day. Nothing daunted us. We travelled, often uncomfortably and on long journeys, to talk with women in other cities about organizing joint campaigns. Along with several other organizations, we formed a collective platform called the Dahej Virodhi Chetna Manch under whose aegis we organized meetings and processions. We participated in meetings with the government when it finally gave in to the demand to change the law on dowry.

As we continued to work, we began to realize that just relying on the law was not enough. Several members of the group shared this feeling and we decided to take the anti-dowry campaign further. We continued to hold demonstrations and marches and to make demands for changes in the law. But at the same time, we set our minds to other things we could do to spread our messages and in the course of extended discussions we came up with the idea of doing a street play on dowry. There was tremendous excitement at this—we thought a play had enormous potential. But of course none of us knew anything about how to put a play together. So we got in touch with a friend, Anuradha Kapur, and she brought in another friend, Maya Rao. Anuradha and Maya scripted the play we eventually put up on the basis of real-life stories of dowry deaths that we told them and those they were familiar with, and we began rehearsals in the house of another friend, Lakshmi Rao, in central Delhi. The back veranda and garden of Lakshmi's father's gracious house provided us ample space for rehearsals.

We would assemble there every day, travelling across the city by bus or scooter rickshaw—none of us was rich enough to take taxis and few of us had cars. Anuradha and Maya would take us through a series of improvisations on the stories we had told them, and bit by bit a final script began to take shape. We were all dedicated and fully committed—I think none of us even felt the tiredness of travel or of the long hours we spent discussing, enacting and writing this or that scene. As I look back on that period today, I wonder how I managed with my job and my household responsibilities and all the time taken for travel. It seemed that in no time— though in reality I know it was at least a month or two— we had our play ready. We called it *Om Swaha* and based it on the lives of Hardeep and Tarvinder, though much of it was fictionalized quite differently from their lives. In the play, Hardeep and Tarvinder are friends—as they were in real life—and while one dies as a victim of dowry, the other decides to fight. At the end, we would often ask the audience what they felt the women should have done and would get many different responses, but always there was sympathy with the women.

Our first performance was at Indraprastha College for Women. Maya Rao had not only co-directed the play but was also one of the actors in it. And Maya is a consummate actor. I still remember the reaction when she played Hardeep's death: we had used red dupattas to simulate flames and weren't sure if this would work. But as Maya's screams rent the air, it was almost as if everything, even the traffic on the roads outside, came to a standstill. Even we—who were familiar with every line and nuance of the play—were moved. I felt my hair stand on edge and almost forgot to come in for my cue, which was directly after this, and which involved singing a song, a sad, tragic song, about how a young woman feels on leaving her parental home to go to a place she does not know to live with people she has never met before.

We took *Om Swaha* all over Delhi and its adjoining areas. We would just meet and decide on where we were going or go where we had been asked to go and would usually take off in a bus, with our dholak and harmonium—we used the dholak to attract people to the play and the harmonium provided accompaniment to our songs. The only other props we had were our black khadi kurtas, purchased out of our meagre earnings, which we used to identify ourselves as members of a theatre troupe. Once at our destination, we would collect a crowd by singing and dancing and would then begin our performance. Everywhere we would hold discussions after the play and it was interesting that men watching the play would always be ready to put the blame on women. 'It's the mother-in-law,' they would say, 'what do we know about these things; we are always out of the house.' Of course mothers-in-law were involved, as were many other male and female relatives. We discovered this over time and learnt gradually to counter their arguments with confidence.

The success of *Om Swaha* spurred us on to other things. We had also become involved in the agitation against rape. When four well-known lawyers protested the Supreme Court's acquittal of two policemen accused of raping a minor girl, Mathura (they had previously been found guilty by the sessions court and the high court), the anti-rape campaign spread all over the country and assumed national dimensions. Along with other groups in Delhi, we too joined this campaign and helped to raise awareness about the issue. We published a number of pamphlets, sent an investigative team to Bihar to look into an incident of gang rape of Dalits there, held a major demonstration on 8 March, international women's day, demanding changes in the law on rape, and helped put together a list of changes that we placed before the Law Commission. Some of the changes were accepted and some rejected (as happened with the changes in the dowry law) when the new law was finally given shape. And throughout this time we staged a street play on rape.

The anti-dowry and anti-rape agitations and the two plays drew a lot of response. Everywhere we went, people would come and tell us about this or that incident that had taken place somewhere. We tried to go to as many of these places as possible, feeling that we would get more of a response if we went to areas where the problem had occurred. Once some of the boys who were working in the play were so angry with the husband of one woman that they actually beat him up. But, this incident apart, we were usually very careful not to get into fights and confrontations.

Meanwhile, *Om Swaha* went through several transformations. As we took it from college to college (one of the areas we targeted), students offered to join us. This enabled some of the older members of the group to move out and the younger ones to take their place. Under Maya and Anuradha's direction, the play was taken over and performed by at least three different groups and in each instance it changed a bit although the basic thrust remained the same.

One of our key actors—he played the role of the bridegroom—was the now well-known television personality, and at that time already more than a budding star, Vinod Dua. Not only in colleges and universities but also in residential areas, Dua was a tremendous hit and a great draw. We took full advantage of this, using his presence to raise serious questions.

One day, while performing *Om Swaha* in south Delhi at a place called Malviya Nagar, we learnt about the tragic death of Kanchan Hardy, whose marriage had apparently been postponed three times because of dowry demands. Kanchan was a very beautiful girl and the young man she married had fallen in love with her and was desperate to marry her, but his family wanted dowry.

Kanchan's parents were not particularly well off and they had already had to suffer considerable economic strain: the wedding had been fixed three times, invitations were printed each time and arrangements made and all that money had gone waste. Finally, the couple married in court. But it did not take Kanchan long to find out that she was not the only woman in her husband's life—he continued to flirt and have relationships with other women. Driven to despair, Kanchan once followed her husband to one of his assignations and managed to catch him red-handed. This was the breaking point. Sunil, her husband, joined hands with his family and started harassing her for money. Fearing for her life, Kanchan went away to her parents' home only to be brought back by her husband and then to suffer death by burning at his hands.

We found this story terribly depressing. As our play travelled from place to place, we found that everywhere we went we heard more and more stories of cruelty, of dowry deaths, of young women whose lives were sacrificed because their parents did not care enough to protect them or offer them a home or because they were unable to meet the persistent demands of the in-laws. We decided we needed to do something more than just taking our play around—clearly there was a need for certain kinds of services, legal aid and counselling. And it was out of this understanding that some of the legal aid and counselling centres in Delhi were born. All of us did not wish to be involved in such work, so while some opted to continue campaigning, others went in for setting up institutions to respond to the need for assistance with the law and for counselling.

We were amazed at the level of ignorance among parents, and indeed among women themselves. But it was heartening that once people knew there was a possibility of finding out more about what they should or should not do they showed an eagerness to do so. It was this that encouraged us to start thinking about setting up legal aid and counselling centres, a step that led many of our activists in different directions.

One of the key institutions that came out of this was Saheli, which began in the garage of one of our members and then moved on from there. Looking back on it now, the move from street-level activism to setting up an institute seems a simple enough process. Yet nothing about it was simple. It was clear that there was a need for a centre (indeed, for many centres) which could take up case work, provide legal aid and counselling. But none of us had much experience in running such an institution. Would we be able to do it? We were not trained lawyers or counsellors, how would we fare here? And where would the money come from? How would such a centre be sustained? Those members of Stree Sangharsh who were more interested in setting up such a centre held long, detailed discussions about the pros and cons of taking such a major step. Eventually Saheli and later other centres were set up. Some of them are still around today although in a much changed form.

Our discussions continued over a long period of time. Unfortunately, not all of them ended on a peaceful note and the unpleasantness and bitterness continued to grow. I began to feel that it was not worth the time and effort it took to get through the meetings and to stay involved and so I decided to opt out. We agreed to remain friends and today, when we meet, many of us laugh at our old tensions and differences. Over time, Stree Sangharsh sort of faded away, and many of the activists involved in it went in different directions. I returned to my family life, my job and my other interests.

The Complicity of Families

Alongside the play, we carried on with our work and responded to calls for help and advice whenever they came. One day Satyarani Chadda telephoned to say that a young woman had been killed in her neighbourhood. We all rushed to the place. The woman's body was still in the house and the father-in-law was standing in the veranda as if waiting for someone. While we were marching up and down raising slogans, a taxi drew up to the house. The man who alighted embraced the father-in-law and together the two men went into the house. Someone whispered that it was the girl's father and that there was something 'fishy' going on between the two men. And sure enough, as we stood there, the father came out of the house and began shouting at us. 'What do you think you are doing?' he said. 'Who asked you women to come here? Go away. I don't need your sympathy or your protests. I know my daughter was arrogant and headstrong. Get out of this place before I do something drastic.'

We had no alternative but to withdraw. Later we talked. We were confused. What should we have done?

We knew we were there fighting for a woman's right, but if someone from her own family insisted we had no right to do this . . . The dilemma was acute: had we been right in withdrawing? We could have called the police, but we knew that legally we had no right, no locus standi, to be there (the Act of 1961 did not give us any right). Later, many years later, we came to understand that it was important to fight for what we believed was right and that we had to try to balance this with whatever support we could give to the people concerned. But at the time we really did not know what to do. And we felt much worse when we learnt that not too long after this incident, the young woman's father married his second daughter to the same man who had killed his first.

Try as I might, I could not get this situation out of my mind. Again and again I thought of the younger sister who had been placed in her dead sister's shoes, with the knowledge of the fate her sister had met. How would she feel doing this? What did her mother have to say? Was there anyone to listen to her? And if she too was killed, would the father have yet another daughter to give to the same man? Hardeep's brother had withdrawn from the case because he had been defeated by all the forces conspiring against him. That was understandable. But here was a father conspiring with the killer of his daughter simply so that he could 'dispose of' another daughter. Were daughters then such a liability?

Strangely enough, we found that in most of the

dowry death cases, parents did not respond with any seriousness to the complaints of their daughters. In Hardeep's case, when her in-laws sent her back to her parents' house, the father invited some of their relatives to see if they could work out a compromise. Accordingly, they all went to Hardeep's in-laws' house bearing gifts and requested her parents-in-law to take her back. In a sense, by doing this, they sent Hardeep to her death—for the in-laws did take her back only to kill her.

When Tarvinder Kaur died four months after her marriage, her brother told me that among the demands her husband had made was an order to deliver the full furniture for his house in the form of a birthday present a day before the marriage. This was done. But when the marriage party came to the house, the first thing the husband-to-be said was, 'Young man, you owe me some money so let us sort out that account before we get on with the ceremonies and rituals.' Raman, Tarvinder's brother, was shocked. He said, 'But it was a question of family prestige and I found myself being almost apologetic when he told me that I had omitted to pay freight charges for the furniture that was sent to his house as a "birthday gift".' After Tarvinder died of burns, her brother was asked why he had been so unfailingly polite to her in-laws when he knew how they had treated her. He said he had never expected that the violence would take such an extreme form. 'After all,' he said, 'every girl has to adjust in her matrimonial home.'

Adjust. That terrible word. It is a horrifying truth that every time a harassed girl comes back to her parents and complains about the ill-treatment meted out to her, the parents advise her to go back and adjust. Why? I have never been able to understand this. Kanchan Chopra went to her parents' home one day and told her brother that she was not willing to go back to her husband because she feared he would kill her. That morning her husband had tried to strangle her but she managed to pull away and escape. Kanchan had a job and she would not have been a financial strain on her parents. In the evening when her husband came to fetch her back from her parents, he seemed contrite. 'I don't know what came over me this morning,' he said, 'please forgive me.' Kanchan's mother had never seen a husband apologizing to his wife. She was touched and tried to persuade her daughter to go back. Kanchan refused. Finally her mother offered to send Kanchan's brother with her, saying, 'If you don't feel safe you can come back with him.' Hardly had Kanchan and her husband entered their home than the husband started to beat her, berating her for having run to her parents' home.

Her brother ran to the police station to lodge a complaint. But he was told that the area of Kanchan's home did not fall in the jurisdiction of that police station. He ran back to Kanchan's home, wanting to take her away. But it was too late. Kanchan was dead. She had been burnt. 'She committed suicide,' he was told.

One afternoon we had a desperate telephone call from a young woman called Pushpa. 'Please come and rescue me,' she cried. We rushed to her home, informing the local police on the way that something was amiss. When we reached the house we saw that Pushpa was being beaten mercilessly. Her brother-in-law was trying to snatch her baby away from her, and Pushpa was clutching on to him fiercely. We forced our way into this confusion and I took the baby from Pushpa and tried to talk to the brother-in-law. He shouted at me, saying this was their private concern and we had no business to intervene. We continued being reasonable: why did they not try to sort things out amicably and if there was a real problem why not go to the courts, why resort to violence? At some point it seemed as if the mother-in-law was convinced by what we said because she decided to wait until we had had a chance to talk to Pushpa's parents as well.

But this was short-lived. It seemed that Pushpa's husband had run away and no one in the family was prepared to listen to reason. We weren't sure what to do. So we decided it would probably be wise to inform the police. When we spoke to them they seemed to be sympathetic and the station house officer (SHO) deputed a man to keep watch on the family. Two days later, when I went back to the police station, I was informed that the girl had been sent back to her parents' home. But it was not long before the parents brought her back, laden with gifts and probably also money, to her married home. I wondered how they could be so insensitive. The police told us that they had tried to get the girl to talk to them about how she was feeling, but she simply refused. She felt betrayed by everyone, including her own parents, and felt that talking would serve no purpose.

Pritam's story was different. Her mother-in-law would not let her sit down on the sofa in her married home. Every time she sat there, her mother-in-law would scream at her, saying she should tell her parents to send 'proper' furniture. When Pritam got married, she had a temporary job, but her parents-in-law did not know that the job was for a short term. Pritam's trouble got worse when she stopped working. Eventually, her in-laws turned her out of the house but kept her six-month-old child back. We got to know about Pritam when a friend of hers came to us asking for help for a young woman who had been thrown out of her home and forcibly separated from her child. We went to the house, taking the police with us. Pritam and her father were there too, begging her mother-in-law to give the child to her. We'd had the sense to take the SHO of the police station with us. He walked over to the mother-in-law and said to her, 'Let me take the child out for a while, away from this noise. I'll bring her back when she has calmed down a bit.' The mother-in-law handed the child over to him. He went outside the house and indicated that I should follow him. Outside, he handed the child over to Pritam who was standing there and said, 'Here, take the child and run. We'll handle the situation inside.' Pritam did not wait to be told twice.

Today, this young child is almost sixteen years old and doing very well. Other things in the family have changed too—I don't know if Pritam's parents reached a compromise with her in-laws or if it was something else, but Pritam is back in her husband's home and she now has a career. For our part, as often happens with women's groups, we lost track of the case after this particular incident because Pritam did not stay in touch with us, and we did not know whether to pursue the case or not. It is this not knowing that often makes things difficult for women's groups, for you start by giving as much support as possible to the person who needs it and trying to make her self-sufficient. But when she feels she is capable of making her own decisions, it is difficult to advice her if you think she is making a 'wrong' decision. Instead, you take a back seat, so to speak, leaving the woman to make her own decisions, while being there to support her whenever she needs support. It's not always easy: I have often felt angry with women who, despite being brutalized by their husbands and others in the worst possible way, and after spending hours discussing their lives with us, go right back into the same violent situation. It has taken me years to realize that there is little we can do about this. In the end, we must leave the woman to take the decision she feels is best—and often this may not be the 'right' decision, but given the circumstances of most women's lives, it is perhaps the only one.

I'm reminded of Lalita's story. She was burnt to death in her husband's house in Rohini, a suburb of Delhi. Her husband was unemployed and he had got used to extracting money from her parents using threats of violence against Lalita (which were often carried out) to intimidate them into complying. Lalita ran a beauty parlour in her home and earned enough to sustain her family. Nonetheless, her husband's demands for money did not stop. After her death, her daughter narrated how her father would constantly beat the mother and abuse her parents for not giving them enough money. Once, when the family had gone to Hardwar for her young son's mundan (head shaving) ceremony, the husband had created a fuss and demanded two lakh rupees. Lalita's mother gave him half the amount, which was all she had, and some jewellery. Dissatisfied, he killed his wife. Afterwards, when the police asked the parents why they did not complain when their daughter was being harassed, Lalita's father said, 'We did not want a divorce. We have another daughter to marry, and a divorce would have meant scandal in the family and the community and it could have affected our chances of finding her a good match.' It is considerations like these, among others, that force many young women to go back to abusive situations.

Parents, relatives and friends of women who are

harassed seldom act in time: they're all worried that doing so will 'spoil relations'. It doesn't seem to count that relations are spoilt already. As long as this remains under wraps, and no one is forced to acknowledge it, they can pretend it did not exist. When Usha Khanna came to our office and complained that her husband had turned her out of the house and had kept her dowry, we asked her whether or not she had reported the matter to the police. She said she had not. We advised her to write a letter to her husband, making a polite mention that her jewellery was in a cupboard in his home and that pending matters being sorted out, the cupboard should be locked. We thought this would help create evidence that the jewellery had been left behind, should the need for such evidence ever arise. Both Usha and her aunt, who had brought her to us, appreciated this suggestion and wondered why no one had given it to them earlier. They both agreed to write.

That evening, an uncle of Usha's paid us a visit. He was furious with us: he accused us of trying to create a rift between his niece and her husband's family. If we show distrust towards them, he said, how will the girl continue to live there? And that is where she must go— there's nowhere else for her. No matter what we said, he was not willing to listen to us. Predictably, Usha never came back to our office nor did she ever get in touch with us. She must have been forced into the realization that decisions to do with her life were not hers to make.

Rather, they rested with her family. This happens so often: families in our society are so much more concerned with their image in the community than with the lives and wishes of women. As far as they are concerned, women do not exist, except as wives of their husbands, even if this step often means sending them to their deaths.

The irony is that the so-called stigma is always attached to the women. Husbands, men, can do what they like. A divorced man is not stigmatized in the same way as a divorced woman. The husband of a murdered woman has any number of women lining up to marry him. Hardeep's husband, for example, was already married before the trial on her murder was over. In another case, by the time the husband and mother-in-law were convicted by the Supreme Court, the man's second wife was already several months pregnant.

A New Location: An Old Problem

In the 1980s we had moved into our house in Gulmohar Park, a somewhat posh residential area in Delhi. At the time, Stree Sangharsh was in an uncertain state, and Karmika still in its infancy. I was trying to decide what to do: I thought—mistakenly, as it turned out—that we wouldn't see much dowry-related violence in an upmarket place like Gulmohar Park and its surrounding areas like Green Park and Hauz Khas (unlike Jangpura, where we had lived earlier) and so perhaps we needed to think of focusing on other things. I soon realized how wrong I was.

One evening I had a phone call from someone I did not know. He simply said, 'In house no 10D a young housewife has been burnt' and he hung up. I did not know where 10D was but I could not sit still. So I went to the police station closest to my home and asked a policeman to direct me to 10D. 'I'm also going there,' he said, 'come with me.' I followed him a little nervously—it was dark, I was new to the place and policemen are not always the most reliable of people. When we reached 10D, there seemed to be no one there and there were no lights either. I waited outside while the policeman went in. I noticed a few women gathered together at a neighbour's house. I went up to them and heard one of them describe how they had all rushed out on hearing the screams of a young woman, Bharati Narula. They said that even as the burning woman was screaming in the yard her father-in-law came out and dragged her into the house. 'It all happened in just fifteen minutes,' they said. The girl was almost totally burnt—100 per cent burns, the hospital later told us—and I could not believe this could have happened in a house full of people. Clearly no one had made any effort to save her.

Like all the others, this case too went to court. The husband, mother-in-law and father-in-law were arrested. When their bail application came up for hearing, the judge asked how it was that a house in such an upper middle-class area had no gas connection? How was it that the girl had been burnt while cooking on a kerosene stove? On the basis of the investigating officer's report (which established that a small kerosene stove was found lying in one corner and the girl's dupatta was there as well, soaked in kerosene oil) the judge refused to give them bail and they were sent to jail. But they were out in a bare four months. During this time their bail application was consistently opposed by the investigating officer but they somehow managed to get bail. It was a very secret affair. Their lawyer knew that if news of their bail leaked out, there would be considerable opposition.

And predictably, the first thing they did when they came out was to pay off the woman who had given evidence.

When I realized what they were attempting, I went to see the woman. I tried hard to persuade her to stand by her word. But she wasn't willing. She said 'You see, I have three grown-up daughters, and as I live in the same neighbourhood I can't afford to antagonize these people. My husband also refuses to allow me to intervene.' I tried everything—arguments, persuasion—but nothing worked. And later we read in the papers that in Bharati Narula's case, as in many others, the witness had 'turned hostile'.

Initially, Bharati's father was extremely upset and was determined to see the case through. But after a number of adjournments he began to lose heart. 'Each time I come for a hearing,' he said, 'I hope the case will make some progress but every time it is adjourned. Or a new judge comes in and says he needs time to understand the background. Or then the counsel falls ill and the hearing is postponed. Each trip to Delhi [he lived in Kaithal, some distance from Delhi] means not only spending money but also taking time off work—sometimes it is as much as three days. And then, I have no place to stay in Delhi, so I have to rent a room . . .' All this was beginning to tell on his health.

He told us how Bharati's father-in-law had demanded a scooter. 'He knew I had given a scooter to my other son-in-law—our wives are sisters, and since our caste allows marriage with cousins, we married Bharati into this family—so he insisted I give him one too. I told him the business was not going well and that I would make sure he had a scooter the moment I had money to spare. But he was not satisfied with that. Around the last time Bharati came to see us she complained to her mother that they were treating her badly because the scooter had not arrived. She did not want to go back— she'd read about so many dowry deaths that she was actually quite frightened. But her mother insisted, saying that she was going back to her own home, to her aunt, what was there to worry about? But she wept as she left. She clung to her brother, saying that she had hoped he would understand, that she knew she would be killed . . . I wish we had listened to her.'

The trial dragged on for several months—perhaps even years. Then the judge was transferred. I tried to follow it for a while, but one day, when I went to court to check on things, I was told that the file pertaining to the case had mysteriously disappeared. The new judge who was brought in said he could not deal with the case because he was not familiar with the details and the police had not made out a proper case. Ultimately, the accused were acquitted. What did it matter after all? It was just another insignificant life—a woman's life—that had gone.

I found this terribly depressing: it seemed that no matter where you turned, the odds were heavily weighed against the woman. Whether it was the family or the law or the investigating authorities or the judiciary, all they seemed to be interested in was saving their own skins, and often making a fast buck in the bargain. The lives of women, their feelings and desires, their aspirations: these counted for nothing at all. In the face of such indifference I alternated between thinking that I should give up any involvement in the anti-dowry agitation and that I needed to work harder at strengthening our group for that was the only way we could have a chance of making some sort of dent.

The Narulas sold their house in Gulmohar Park for a hefty amount and moved to a newly built flat. Bharati's husband married again, bought a new car and forgot all about the wife who had been burnt to death. The residents of Gulmohar Park who had launched a month-long protest finally ended up sending a letter to the then prime minister, Indira Gandhi, suggesting measures that could be done to curtail the rising incidence of dowry deaths. Here is the text of the letter.

The Honourable Prime Minister
Prime Minister's Secretariat
New Delhi

Dear Madam Prime Minister
While India is registering growth in other sectors on the women's welfare front we note with deep concern that this increasing prosperity has, in fact, unleashed

a new wave of violence against women. The growing incidence of dowry deaths is alarming and we feel that unless the sternest measures are taken to stem this tide, India's dowry deaths might become an international scandal.

We therefore appeal to you as leader of the country to take the following steps to curtail this social evil.

1. All newspapers carrying matrimonial advertisements should compulsorily carry a box stating in capital letters: DOWRY IS AN OFFENCE PUNISHABLE BY IMPRISONMENT or BEWARE OF DOWRY HUNTERS WHO WANT DOWRY AND NOT YOUR DAUGHTER/WARD. Already a statutory warning about cigarettes has to be published alongside all cigarette advertisements.

2. Each state government and the Delhi Administration should have a Dowry Harassment Monitoring cell which would pursue dowry cases including murders and abetment to suicide making sure that they are speedily taken up. This cell should have four or five focal points and the names of such focal points along with their addresses and telephone numbers should be widely publicised. Aggrieved parties could contact these cells and seek redress.

3. Where there is suspicion that the parents of the girl are not alive or are not in a position to take her back, the husband and in-laws should be bound to good behaviour under section 108CPC.

4. In extreme cases the woman should be removed to a shelter to be opened for this purpose and effort be made to get her a divorce if necessary and other measures adopted to rehabilitate her. Such a home should have the assistance of women police and social workers.

5. Section 106 CPC should be suitably amended to ensure that those who ill-treat their wives to the extent of driving them to suicide are duly punished. Any demand for money or things from the bride's family be construed as abetment to suicide.

6. In case of any unnatural death of a bride within five or six years of marriage, the burden of proof should be on the husband and the in-laws.

7. Photographs of the accused and other particulars of their profession etc. should be published in newspapers and the television and if circumstantial evidence weighs heavily against them, their professional licence should be cancelled. Those in employment should be suspended the moment a complaint is lodged against them. If convicted, they should be permanently debarred.

8. All trials of dowry murder cases should be time bound and special courts be set up for the purpose.

On behalf of Karmika, a voluntary organization, Women's Club Gulmohar Park, the Gulmohar Park Welfare Society, the YWCA, the All India Women's Conference, I appeal to you to consider these proposals. We shall be grateful if you can spare some time to have a discussion with us on this subject.

We had drafted this letter in the hope that we would get some kind of response from the prime minister. But all we got, disappointingly, was a deafening silence. This from a prime minister who had time and again expressed her concern for Indian women! But we did not lose courage and kept up our agitation. We went to Narula's boss and demanded that he be dismissed from his job. He didn't agree, of course, saying that Narula had not been in his employ for too long, but he said he would try to get him to retire voluntarily. This he did, which we took as a small victory which compensated, at least in some measure, for the prime minister's indifference.

Whether or not our agitation had anything to do with it I do not know, but soon after the Law Commission undertook a review of the existing law on dowry to suggest amendments and improvements. A select committee was set up to look into this and its members travelled all over the country, assessing the situation, interviewing individuals and meeting activist groups. They spent two years studying the law and its implementation and came up with a detailed report containing a list of suggestions for change. However, once the report was in, the government was not particularly interested in taking things further. It was only under considerable pressure from non-governmental organizations (NGOs) that the report was put before the house. One of the things the committee/Law Commission pointed out was that the definition of dowry in the Act of 1961 was faulty and open to misinterpretation and misuse. They suggested that the definition needed to be more comprehensive, something which the lawmakers ignored in their usual cavalier manner. Many other suggestions made by the Law Commission were dropped. We were disappointed at this of course but it gave us some comfort to see that we were not the only ones to face indifference.

Building an Institution

At some stage—I'm not quite sure when—Stree Sangharsh began to fade into the background for me, to be replaced by Karmika. When it seemed unlikely that Stree Sangharsh would continue, some of us began to think of setting up another organization. For the first few years of its existence, Karmika, like Stree Sangharsh, remained a loose body of a few women and we operated informally from my house. The founding group was made up of women from different professions and, very soon, some of them who were government servants wanted to opt out because they found that they were forbidden to join any organization that could be seen as 'political'. We had consciously thought of ourselves as non-political and had refused to affiliate with any political party, but for the government, any whiff of work with women seemed to be political and so these women had to withdraw.

Until this time, Karmika had had no fixed address. But we needed a place to work from if we were to take up counselling and legal aid properly, and we needed to maintain records, bring in new members, find money to function and so on. Since much of the activity around the Bharati Narula case had taken place in Gulmohar Park, several women from this area became interested in joining us. One of them, Saraswati Venkatasubbiah, generously offered a room over her garage as an office and gave us some of her surplus furniture to put into it. Within a short while we were in full swing: we organized talks, film shows, seminars and discussions and we were available eight hours a day for anyone who came in for counselling and legal aid. My friend Chandar, a lawyer who worked with us, gave generously of her time and because of her a number of younger lawyers offered to help us out.

Working within an institutional framework has its ups and downs. In Stree Sangharsh, I had often found that the endless discussions, the extra care taken to avoid hierarchies (although they always crept in anyway) and the painstaking attempts at maintaining democratic functioning were extremely frustrating. This is what had prompted me to work in a different way in Karmika—not particularly hierarchical, but without any ambivalence about who took decisions and where responsibility lay. We also needed to employ counsellors and researchers to work with us and for this we needed money. Because we were a registered organization and had permission to receive foreign funds, we were able to access some small amounts of money from one or two organizations for running our office (although most of our people were voluntary workers). But we also thought we should turn, like other NGOs, to our own ministries and departments for funds. After all, working for the betterment of women's status was as much their responsibility as ours.

But this was easier said than done. Government grants come with so many strings attached and are so tied up in bureaucracy that you might as well not have them. First you need to apply in particular formats, then you need to prove several things, then you almost need to beg for money that should rightfully be yours (for after all, it has come from the taxes we pay), and often you have to pay bribes to get it, then you never receive the money in time (I now realize this is a deliberate tactic) or you never receive the full amount. And as if all this was not enough, the money, when it is finally paid, is meagre. To give just one example: we had applied to the Central Social Welfare Board for funds for appointing counsellors to our family counselling unit. We were sanctioned a grant that allowed us to pay only Rs 2500 as salary to each counsellor. But the grant conditions also specified that any person we appointed should have a minimum qualification of a master's degree in the social sciences or psychology, as well as at least two years of field experience. State institutions seem to have never asked themselves why anyone with this kind of background and qualification would work for less than the minimum wage. I cannot count the number of times we tried to discuss this with the Central Social Welfare Board and tried to make them understand that such a wage was simply too low, but to no avail. There were times when we were lucky and we did manage to appoint people who were willing to work despite the low wage, but understandably, they would stay for a short while and leave the moment they got a better chance. But such occasions were rare. While dealing with the government, if we were not chasing them for more money, we were chasing them to fulfil their existing, albeit meagre, commitments. To get them to do even this was virtually impossible.

Nonetheless, despite these hurdles, our work was slowly beginning to take shape. We were a small core of women, we had defined ourselves as an organization that would provide legal aid and counselling to women (or their families) victims of violence, particularly domestic violence. For the most part, the cases that we dealt with related to dowry, but we did on occasion get other cases of violence within the home or of harassment in the workplace. To do this effectively, we needed to have a formal structure and a few lawyers on board who would be willing to take on cases for free or at a reduced cost. We also needed to maintain records to reassure people that we had both solidity and sustainability. For this, we needed to register ourselves, to work out of an office rather than informally in someone's home. But we had no money, and so we thought of doing what other women's groups had done, which was to try and ask the Delhi administration to give us office premises. At the time, the Lieutenant Governor of Delhi was Jagmohan, who was known to be an accessible man. Various friends in the government advised us to approach him, so we gathered our courage together and went to see him.

The first question Jagmohan asked us—after granting us a patient and sympathetic hearing—was whether we had any money. We said we didn't have much. 'How do you manage your expenses?' he asked. We explained that we ran the office on donations from friends and well-wishers and that, as and when it was necessary, we put in our own money. He took our application and suggested we see a place in south Delhi where another women's organization, Saheli, was also housed.

Thinking it might be better to be closer to our place of work and also that it was probably not a good idea for all women's organizations to be in the same area, we asked if we could look elsewhere. 'All right,' he said to us, 'some new shops have been constructed in the Green Park area. Take a look at those and come and tell me.'

We were happy and hopeful. The next day we looked around and identified a few shops in Green Park and Neeti Bagh, both areas that were close to where our work was concentrated. But at that point our luck ran out. Before we could get back to him, Jagmohan was transferred out of Delhi. We were dispirited, but decided not to give up and approached the new Lieutenant

Governor, H.K.L. Kapoor. He advised us to follow all the steps the bureaucracy requires you to follow: get a form from the Delhi Development Authority (DDA), fill it up, get a government recommendation to support our claim and then submit it to him. All this took a little time, but we managed it, with a bit of help. At the time, the minister for women's development was Margaret Alva, who was very approachable, and her Joint Secretary, C.P. Sujayya, was also equally helpful. So we had no difficulty in getting the necessary recommendations. Little did we realize, when we handed in our papers, that we were digging a pit of sorrow for ourselves. The mad round of dealing with the bureaucracy, its inefficiency, its corruption, its total rottenness and of dealing with the courts—equally corrupt, open to bribery, rotten through and through—now began. Of course, like all such things, it began slowly and we did not recognize what was happening. In hindsight, I can now see that many years of my life were wasted in a fruitless battle with the Indian bureaucracy and the Indian courts. I realized, as the years went by, that I was now getting a taste, albeit in a different way, of what women who were victims of dowry were confronted by: an indifferent, sometimes downright prejudiced system, endemic corruption, obdurate officials and criminals masquerading as politicians. But let me tell the story as it happened. It took twelve long years during which we continued to work, moving from place to place in rented premises, and it took a heavy toll on us.

Once our application was in with the authorities, we were advised to see the commissioner of lands whose office is located inside an august building called Vikas Sadan. We went and found, not surprisingly, that the commissioner was seldom available. He would either be called away to 'an important meeting' or he would be busy with 'VIPs'. I spent several Mondays and Thursdays in that crowded waiting room, awaiting the commissioner's personal assistant's (PA) nod.

Once again, a small piece of luck came our way: the Lieutenant Governor got himself a new Personal Secretary (PS) and he turned out to be someone I knew. I asked him for help and he suggested that the next time I was in the waiting room, I should just send in a little slip with his name on it. I did, and it had the desired effect—the commissioner's attitude began to change. We were shown a chart of a shopping centre close to our area of work and told that four large office rooms were vacant there; we could see them if we were interested. We went immediately. As the rooms were perfect for our work, we went back to the commissioner and indicated our willingness to take them on. Now that we had something concrete in hand, we started to look for money. We approached donors and the Department of Women and Child Development, the latter to recommend that the rent be lowered since we were a non-profit social work organization. Once again, they were helpful and immediately provided us the necessary recommendations. Meanwhile, the DDA did its usual trick and quietly started backing out of the offer.

At first, the four rooms were reduced to two. Then it came down to one. I went back to the commissioner to ask him why this had happened. He was arrogant, and angry. 'Who authorized you to discuss the matter with my junior?' he demanded. While the negotiations were going on, we had been in touch with someone else in his office because he was never available and we did not think we needed to bother him with the details. We were advised by the office staff to deal with one person, and that is who we dealt with. And now, here was the boss, furious because he thought we had bypassed him! I tried to tell him that we had all along been interacting with 'his junior' but he would have none of it. He told me in no uncertain terms to get out of his office. 'I don't want to hear this nonsense,' he said, 'get out, get out of my office.' I swallowed the insult and my anger. Everything in me was screaming to call him a bloody fool in my usual manner and perhaps to punch him in the face, but I told myself bureaucrats have fragile egos and I should exercise restraint, so I did.

I walked out fuming. A slip of a man, I thought, and so arrogant. Today, when I think back on the incident, I laugh. Imagine feeling offended because the man was small rather than because of what he said (though there was that too). But I did not leave things there: I went to Margaret Alva and then to the Lieutenant Governor. He was apologetic. I guessed that he was offended with his officer and perhaps he wasn't particularly happy with him anyway. Shortly afterwards, the man was transferred to another department—the government's way of punishing its officers is always to transfer them.

By this time we had become more realistic. We thought, even if we were down from four rooms to one, we should not let the opportunity go by so we showed our willingness to take up that one room. The room had a large open terrace on one side and it would be quite useful for our work. One morning we were informed that the allotment letter was ready and we should go with a draft of Rs 45,000 as advance payment. So we rushed to the bank, got a draft made and went to collect our letter of allotment. Predictably, we were made to shuttle from one officer to the other and back again, but finally we did succeed in getting the letter from them.

I don't know what it was, but something made me read the letter carefully before handing over the money to them. I could not believe my eyes. It was sheer fraud. We had been promised room no. 4, which was a large, spacious room with an attached toilet and a terrace, and the letter mentioned a much smaller room, also numbered 4, on the ground floor but it was less than half the size of the original room. Both my lawyer colleague, Chandar, and I looked at the letter in shock and horror.

We rushed to the office of the additional commissioner, lands, and he seemed equally shocked. 'This is impossible, someone must have made a typing error,' he said. He called another officer, one Puri, and instructed him to get the letter corrected. 'They were allotted no. 4,' he said, 'please get this letter corrected.'

But Puri looked everywhere except at his senior officer. He shuffled his feet, and then, when he felt confident enough to open his mouth he said, 'I am sorry sir, but unit no. 4 has . . . er . . . been sold. It was a mistake sir, but . . .' There was nothing to be said after that. We picked up our papers, returned their fraud letter to them, took our draft along and left, empty-handed and disillusioned. Later, when we recounted the story to the Lieutenant Governor, he said, 'I am ashamed, but the DDA is a very corrupt department.'

Coming from the chairman of the DDA, this was a devastating statement. It didn't help us though. But then he suggested that we apply for a small piece of land on which to build and said he would help with that. So we did, little knowing that we were putting our feet deeper into the mire. It took more than a year but we got our allotment finally, and by the time it came we had also managed to get some funds (mainly from the Norwegian development agency NORAD) to build ourselves a small office. All set now, we got ourselves an architect, had plans drawn up and approved, went through all the formalities required by the DDA (and there were plenty) as well as the Municipal Corporation of Delhi (MCD) and, in January 1990, we got ready to start the building.

We'd organized a small ceremony to inaugurate the construction. We invited friends and our co-workers. Our celebration had barely begun when a large crowd of hoodlums swooped down upon us, brandishing lathis. They upturned our tables, threw all the food on to the ground, threatened to beat up our guests and generally created mayhem. We were quite unprepared for all this and had no idea where it was coming from. Our builders beat a hasty retreat and left us women to deal with the situation. Among the crowd was one man, presumably their leader. I tried to talk to him, to show him all our papers, but he was obdurate and his followers abusive. So we gave up trying to put some sense into their heads and instead went to report to the police. They acted reasonably promptly, but the damage had already been done, and the hoodlums had melted away.

Another long ordeal now began. The DDA advised us time and again to build a boundary wall around our property but every time we made an attempt to do so, a crowd would collect and start throwing stones. Our repeated requests for help from the police failed to get any response. It took us a while to understand that this was not a simple protest at a piece of land being sold to someone, rather there were political powers behind it. Most of our opponents were supporters of the Bharatiya Janata Party (BJP) and they had the support of a number of BJP MLAs. This was to be confirmed by later developments.

All the while this was happening, we continued to work to get our building plan ready for submission for clearance. We now took it to the Town Hall to hand it in and were surprised when they refused to accept it. No reason was given but in the way that these things often emerge, we were told by someone that they had had express instructions from Madan Lal Khurana, a BJP leader, to turn our plan down. So, innocently, we thought we should meet Khurana and I asked a friend of my husband's, in whose house Khurana had sought shelter during the Emergency, to help. We were given an appointment immediately.

At Khurana's house we were received with great ceremony and all other visitors were put aside because of us. We were offered sweets and other refreshments. Mr Khurana came in, seemingly in a good mood. We showed him our papers. He professed himself very annoyed and said he would see to it that no further trouble came to us. 'They are liars,' he said about the people at the Town Hall. 'They misinformed me. I'll see to it that everything is OK.'

Later developments proved the hollowness of his promise. Nothing happened, except further trouble from the MCD. They accepted the building plan, albeit reluctantly, but clearly our opponents had a 'mole' in the MCD, for very soon we found we had a court case slapped against us. But not before they came to us and asked if we were willing to give them half the land, or at least half the cost of the land, in the event of which they would withdraw the case. 'This is prime land,' said their leader who came to discuss things with me. 'We know you've got it at a subsidized price. Why shouldn't we have a share of it?'

The first time I received the court summons I was extremely disturbed. Later, summonses became routine and they did not bother me so much. But the first time is always a shock. Part of my worry was that I knew of no reliable lawyer whom I could entrust with the case. Our experience of the law courts and of lawyers had shown that they were not only corrupt but also only interested in making quick money. Clients, they seemed to say, be hanged, as long as we can get our money out of them. And we had precious little money to spend on litigation. Anyway, we went from lawyer to lawyer and, finally, after years (it would be too tedious to explain the many hoops we jumped through) we got someone who has stayed with us and has been totally honest and helpful—a rare and precious thing.

We were in the lower courts for a year, at the end of which the case was decided in our favour. During this time, the MCD approved our building plan. But even as this was going on, Madan Lal Khurana, for reasons best known to himself, gave a statement in the papers that the DDA had illegally allotted a piece of land to an NGO called Karmika. The newspapers lapped this up of course, but luckily the judge ignored the newspaper reports while giving his judgement.

From the lower court the case moved to the high court where, after much to-ing and fro-ing and a lot of dishonest deposing, the matter came to a head when the DDA deposed before the high court that they had identified another plot which they wished to give us in lieu of the one we had already paid for and taken possession of. I thought, all right, if this is the only solution, we'll go for this. But of course months passed and nothing happened. Once again, I decided to beard the lion in his den and went to see the vice-chairman of the DDA. After two or three security checks, I was let into the air-conditioned offices of the vice-chairman and shortly afterwards I was called in. The vice-chairman was busy on the telephone and gestured to me to sit down. Once he was through he asked, 'Yes, what is your case?'

I was surprised. I thought officials usually read up for appointments they make but clearly I was mistaken. Nonetheless, I launched patiently into an explanation. Barely had I begun than the phone rang. 'Put him through,' he said to his factotum at the other end, and, as the other person came on the line, 'Oh, helloooo, you lucky man, you have been to John Major country, breaking and making ministries and here we are burning in this cursed heat!' This was followed by a guffaw. 'Why don't you come over for dinner one of these days? How is Chitra?' Guffaw. 'Yaar, here I was, so happy and enjoying my stint in environment and now look at this . . .' The conversation went on for about five minutes while I sat and waited. Once he was done, he turned to me without a word of apology (I suppose bureaucrats don't need to be polite) and asked me to go on.

I started all over again. He interrupted, 'Excuse me, but who are you representing?' I thought this was amazing but I did not let it bother me and quickly told him about the case. Even as I was finishing the phone rang again. Another friend. This time the conversation— looong like his hellooo—related to a celebration which officers of the Rajasthan cadre were planning. He gave instructions and suggested something about a VIP they wanted to invite and it went on endlessly. A few minutes later, as I left his office, his PA followed me and asked for details of the case. Innocently, I explained everything to him. Later, my advocate told me that PAs usually follow people when they want a bribe. I wasn't asked for one though. Anyway, predictably nothing happened, except that the DDA wrote me a letter to say that if I agreed to accept an alternative plot, they would put it before their screening committee, and then the committee, in its wisdom, would see whether or not they could grant me a plot. I realized then that the DDA authorities think they are the only ones who have any intelligence. No person in her right mind would be fooled by such a stratagem. I certainly wasn't.

Bureaucrats weren't the only ones who behaved like this. I remember making several appointments with an advocate (not the one I have referred to above, but a senior counsel who was supposed to have a lot of clout) we had hired and trying to meet him. Each time, I was treated like dirt. There were no chairs on which clients could sit and wait, there was no respect for time and the only time advocates showed any interest in anything was when they were demanding grossly inflated fees. I have suffered this so many times that I would willingly do serious damage to the lawyer community if I could!

Anyway, just as there were many false starts and hopes in our long and arduous journey through the courts and the bureaucracy so also were there many times when, the case being decided in our favour, we decided to try and go ahead with the building. I remember one particular instance. I had been in touch with a senior police officer in south Delhi. He advised me not to start work on a Friday as that was the day of namaz and they needed an extra police force to keep watch. I was surprised that you needed extra police to watch over people who were praying, but I agreed. This time round, we had been more careful—instead of trying to build with bricks and mortar, we had got ourselves a prefabricated cabin and we planned to just put that up, leaving the real building activity till later. So we got our contractor and he got his workers, and our architect promised to be back and, on the appointed day, I was getting ready to leave for the site when two policemen arrived at my house. 'We suggest,' they said, 'that you go back to the vice-chairman of the DDA.' I asked them why, after all we were in the right. We had paid for our plot, had our plans approved and so on. The police were furious with me—I'm sure they were thinking what right does this woman have to defy us. I was quite nervous but I put up a brave front because I knew I had the backing of their senior officer.

But I couldn't have been more wrong—and I should have known better. Just then, the telephone rang. The officer was on the line. He too advised me to go to the vice-chairman of the DDA. 'Why?' I asked him. He didn't give me a reason, but he told me quite clearly that he had got a message from the chief minister's office that Karmika was not to be allowed to build and that the chief minister had asked the DDA to allot us another piece of land. What right had he to decide this on our behalf, I wondered, becoming even more stubborn and determined to fight. I think all the men I encountered along the way in this long struggle were just so taken aback at the idea of a woman fighting for her rights that they became equally determined not to give in. At times I could not figure out what their interest was in making obstacle after obstacle for us. It wasn't that we were asked for bribes—except for the occasional instance of such a demand, for the most part, people did not demand money—but they just did not like the fact that we were willing to put up a fight.

What with all these hurdles and the constant running to and from the courts, we began to feel a total sense of despair in our office. This piece of land, the office and community centre we hoped to build on it were meant to assist us in our work with women. We'd naively believed that no one—the courts, the police, the bureaucracy, the lawyers—could have any objection to what we were doing, but clearly we were wrong. It took all our energy and strength to keep the office going and to continue working even as we chased people all over to get our land back. Apart from anything else, we had paid for this piece of land and it belonged to us. Those who were fighting us for it had neither paid for it nor did they intend to. They simply thought that the political protection they had would give them all the privileges such protection does and they'd get the land for free. As for the BJP which was supporting them, they quite clearly believed that keeping a vote bank happy was a more laudable motive than working for the benefit of women. Who cared for women anyway? I don't want to go into the painful details of the court cases, but I learnt at every step that judges too had their price. Lawyers spoke openly about this: this one, they said, belongs to such and such party; this one takes so much money. Apart from this the courts don't work in the summer, because lawyers need time off to spend all the money they have made and judges go on foreign trips. Those seeking legal redress—well, who cares for them anyway? So much for justice.

At the time of writing, the case has been in court for twelve years. During this time, we in Karmika continued to work with women, but clearly a great deal of our energy (especially mine) went into this court case. After a few years, we were all tired of it and were quite willing to give up our claim on the place, as long as the DDA returned our money so that we could buy another place of our choosing. However, even for that, we need to go through another long legal process, for how can one expect an organization as corrupt as the DDA to actually return someone's money? I'm now a little over eighty years old. The better part of my life has been spent fighting this fruitless case. But who will be answerable for these wasted years? Activists who wish to work seriously with women are few and far between, and for those who are there it's clear things are not easy. Will we finally win the case, which has been all the way from the lower courts, to the high court, to the Supreme Court and back again? Your guess is as good as mine.

Nonetheless, these twelve years have not been entirely wasted. There are times when I think, well, so much for my belief that things work better if you have an institution to work from. But at least now I understand better the frustration and anger of people who have to deal with the courts. The sad truth is that there is no other system available to us. It's true that there is a need for campaigning and raising public awareness, but for those people whose need is for counselling or legal aid, or both, it is important that there be women's groups and organizations that provide the service and expertise. During this time, we took a small place on rent and have continued and expanded our work from there. I still live in the hope that one day the land that we legally own will be ours and we will be able to build a permanent space for Karmika where women in distress can come when they need help. As a dream, it's a modest one, and one that I hope to realize in my lifetime.

Encounters with the Judiciary

In July 1985 I was asked to appear before the judge in a criminal suit filed against me. I was quite baffled. I hadn't, to my knowledge, committed a crime or even anything remotely resembling one. I asked the bailiff what it was about. But he said he knew nothing. The notice was bailable but if I failed to appear before the judge an arrest warrant would be issued against me. I would also have to furnish security to obtain bail.

On the appointed day I reached the criminal court with my daughter Urvashi who was to stand guarantee for me. I had to wait in the criminal court in the company of a number of criminals of different categories, none of them very pleasant people. While I sat there feeling uncomfortable, I wondered what it was I had done. This—the waiting amid others in handcuffs or bedraggled from being in custody—was an experience I did not want to repeat.

Later, when my advocate arrived, I learnt that the case against me was one of defamation filed by the father-in-law of a young woman called Shobha Gandhi. Shobha's story had completely escaped my mind, so it took me a while to remember the case. She had come to me to get her dowry recovered. In fact, she had been brought to me by Chandar, our friend and advocate.

Shobha's marriage had failed before it had even taken off. Her parents, rich business people of Bombay, did not want her to marry someone of her own choosing. 'In our community,' said her mother, 'we don't allow our girls to select their own husbands. It is the duty of the parents and only they can tell what is good for their children.' Shobha had actually accepted her parents' decision although she was keen to marry someone else. Shortly after their marriage, her husband came to know about her friendship with the other man and made an issue of it. This is what she said, 'He asked me what kind of relationship I had had with him. I thought I should be honest so I told him that I had wanted to marry him but since my parents did not want me to do so, I had given in to their decision. He was angry and began to shout and scream. He said he had been cheated and that he would go to the court and seek a divorce. He had taped everything that I had told him though all the time I kept insisting that the other man and I had just been friends, which was the truth. However, on the basis of the recording he filed a divorce petition in the court which was rejected. But since he decided to separate from me, I asked him to return the dowry my parents had given to me. He refused. I was very unhappy. I hadn't been able to marry the person I wanted to, and I could not get any love or understanding from the man I was married to. And now he was even refusing to return my dowry. My parents are unhappy that I have confessed the truth because now they feel humiliated in society. My husband is angry because I had a boyfriend before I married him and he wants to reject me but to hold on to all my belongings. He does not see anything wrong in that; presumably he sees that as his right. But what about my rights?'

Shobha was angry and she had asked for our help in getting her things back. She was not interested in chasing 'that man', as she called him. We decided to take the help of the police. Shobha's in-laws lived in north Delhi, so we approached the local police there. They talked to Shobha and questioned her in detail. They seemed to be quite sympathetic and asked her to put in an application for the recovery of her dowry, which would enable them to act. The officer also advised me not to put my name to the application but to let it come from Shobha. After this we were to wait to hear from him, and it could take several hours before he got back to us. Four days later he called to say their team was ready and could we reach his office, but quietly, without telling anyone, since surprise was their weapon against the other party.

We followed his advice. Shobha, Chandar and I arrived at the office of the DCP North on the appointed day. From there, we moved silently towards Shobha's married home, the police party following close on our heels. We felt like soldiers on the warpath, except that we were women and we had no weapons. But victory was not such an easy affair. Even though we had managed to keep the whole operation secret, we met with strong resistance. Within minutes the whole family had collected; Shobha's father-in-law came out with a huge iron rod threatening that anyone who dared to enter would be hit on their heads. This was not what we had expected, and apparently it wasn't what the police expected either, as they went back to their headquarters.

A little while later the police returned with reinforcements and a written order that allowed them to break open the house in the event of resistance. Meanwhile more relatives had arrived and perhaps it had a quietening effect, for the resistance seemed to be wearing thin. At this point the police made one more attempt to enter the house and this time they succeeded. They called Shobha in and asked her to identify her things. Her father then brought a car and everything Shobha had identified was loaded on to it. We made our own list. Everything was to be taken to court and lodged there, where it was to stay until orders could be given for the family to take the things away.

The entire exercise took more than twelve hours and at the end of it Chandar and I were completely exhausted. The day had been hot, adding to our tiredness. We hadn't had anything to eat and had barely managed a cold drink, so we were now ready to go home and collapse. We were standing out on the road looking for transport when Shobha's father came up and offered us a ride, which we gratefully accepted. On the way home he bought some fruit which he offered us and for this too we were grateful. Although we were quite clear that what we were doing was voluntary work—Chandar is a highly paid lawyer but she did this kind of thing for free—we were often struck by how indifferent parents were once the 'task' they had set us on was done. Perhaps indifference is not the right word—they were probably too immersed in their own grief to wonder whether we were hungry or if we could afford to travel to far off places for this work. None of the work we were doing could possibly be free— we spent our own money on transport (there were no funders around in those days and until they made their appearance we had never thought of them as a possible source of money), food and drink, but not once do I remember anyone offering to compensate us or even to contribute to our women's group, at least not voluntarily. When we asked them, they were often very willing to make a contribution, but if we didn't ask, they didn't think of it.

The next morning my friend Sujaya, a government officer well known for her sensitivity to women's issues, called and said, 'You are in the news today.' That was when I found that the newspapers had reported the case and had mentioned my name. Oddly enough, Shobha's father-in-law was greatly upset at the report because, he said, he was a man of high standing and it was humiliating for him to find his name in the papers in this way. I was both surprised and amused to note that the question of 'high standing' and his feelings of humiliation seemed to have come up only when the woman fought back. He had not seemed particularly worried about high standing and feelings of humiliation when his son had tried to kill his wife and grab her belongings or when he turned her out of the house, not even giving her the grace to hold on to her dignity.

But I was not unduly worried about the newspaper report. Such things were routine: we often went out to help people recover their dowry and we would mainly be observers while the police did their job. Recently, I'd been involved in a similar case in Chittaranjan Park in south Delhi with my friend Lotika Sarkar, a well-known lawyer, and the two of us had waited till the police had recovered the woman's belongings and then come away. We hadn't tried to hide our identities from anyone there, and there hadn't been any backlash. In this case, however, Shobha's enraged father-in-law filed a suit against me; so angry was he that he filed both a civil case and a criminal case. His intention was, of course, just to harass me, to make sure that I would spend my time running from one court to the other.

I was quite disturbed by this. I did not relish the prospect of constant running from court to court. I hadn't asked for my name to be mentioned in the news report;

why couldn't the journalists have left it out? What annoyed me more was that the court took such strong notice of something that had appeared in a newspaper, knowing how unreliable newspaper reports are. But courts and judges have their own ways and we can't say anything against them, otherwise we are liable to be hauled up for contempt.

The civil case was over and done with soon. The judge asked only two questions: was the dowry recovered? Who had helped in recovering it? And then he dismissed the case. It was the criminal one that dragged on and on. Even after fourteen years, it had not been resolved. During this time, the advocate who was handling the case on my behalf disappeared without any notice. This isn't unusual: sometimes advocates are bought over by the other side, sometimes they begin to feel there is nothing in the case and it is not worth pursuing but, more often than not, they realize they have earned enough out of a particular case and decide it is not worth putting in any more effort. They are their own masters and the law does not enforce any discipline on them. If they feel a particular judge does not pander to their demands they will boycott him or her or get their union to do so, or worse still go on strike and paralyse the system. Frequent dealings with lawyers open your eyes to the corruption and rot within the legal system, show how completely lacking in ethics and principles they are and how little it matters to them to be fair and just to the people they purport to represent. All that seems to interest them is money and how much of it they can make by dragging cases out—and justice can go hang.

Since I was now without a lawyer—and the unfortunate thing is that the system is such you cannot do without them—I handed over my case to my office lawyer, even though he does not specialize in criminal matters. At least he would have some sense of commitment to it. He is part of an outfit which deals with all branches of law. In the beginning I had to appear on every date the case was called and that can be very tiring and time consuming because in the lower courts you never know when your case is coming up. And so you just sit and wait. Later, I managed to get exempted from appearing and my lawyer appeared on my behalf.

In 1985, as I've mentioned, my daughter stood guarantee for me and I was granted bail. Theoretically, I am still on bail. In the meanwhile, Shobha's father-in-law, who filed the case, died. Shobha and her husband have got a divorce, and both have remarried and have children. Many judges have come and gone, but I continue to be on bail as the case drags on. Shobha's father-in-law has been replaced by her brother-in-law so that the case can continue. So much for the integrity of the judiciary of India. The lawyer who appears for the other side has a very clear strategy to maintain his income level. 'I can manage to get adjournments,' he says. 'One adjournment puts the matter off by five or six months.

The next time I report sick or make an excuse that someone has died or some such thing. Another adjournment. In the meanwhile, the judge changes and a new one comes in and then he needs time to understand the case.' And so it goes on.

It matters little to me. When new incumbents to the high posts of the judiciary make many declarations and express their determination to expedite the procedures of the courts so that the backlog is cleared, I often wonder how much they really mean. Or perhaps they say the right thing only to get some mileage out of it. The miracle of expeditious justice is still a distant dream in independent India.

Satyarani, whose case I have spoken of earlier, is still struggling for justice. Her case did not move out of the trial court for more than ten or twelve years after she filed it. No wonder then that when we suggest to people that they take the case to court, they just laugh and look sceptical. They tell us that the courts are only for the rich who can go on paying and who do not feel the pinch. Like Satya, Parveen Rana's parents too had to spend years waiting for justice. She had been found strangled to death in her husband's house and the case went to Patiala House, where the high court is located, for trial. It took six years to establish whether it was a dowry case or not. In the meanwhile, three judges of Patiala House were transferred and every time a new judge came in, he took time to understand the intricacies of the case. Or at least that is what they said. By the time he had managed to understand it—and this could sometimes take several months—he would be transferred and then the whole process would have to begin all over again. As far as the victim's families are concerned, the system is weighed against them because their case is represented by the state lawyer, who, because he or she is not paid by the aggrieved party, does not really care for them or their priorities. This is why parents feel they are battering their heads against a stone wall and they often give up out of sheer frustration.

Once again, in the 1980s, I received a summons from the court. This time my offence was contempt of court, which seemed to be more serious than the earlier criminal one. I was accused of contempt because I had been rather outspoken in my condemnation of a high court judgement in a dowry case, that of a woman called Sudha Goel who had, like countless other women, been burnt to death in her married home. At the time she was killed, Sudha had almost come to term in her pregnancy and had a nine-month-old fetus in her womb. At the trial court level, the judge, S.M. Aggarwal, condemned Sudha's murderers to death by hanging. But the high court struck down this judgement and, worse, they passed strictures on the judge.

Sudha had lived with her husband and his family in a flat in Delhi, among hundreds of other similar flats. On the fatal night in December, her cries rent the air.

Sudha was being burnt inside her home. As neighbours rushed to her flat, they found they could not get in because the entrance door was bolted from the inside and someone, later identified as her brother-in-law, was putting additional pressure on the door by leaning against it from the inside and holding the latch so it could not be moved. When the neighbours finally managed to push the door in and enter, they saw Sudha in flames, her husband and mother-in-law sitting in the next room, making no attempt to put out the fire.

When Sudha saw the neighbours she shouted out to them, 'These people have killed me, they have taken my gold and everything.' She recognized one of the neighbours whom she knew as Bobby's mother, and called out to her, 'Bobby's mummy, Bobby's mummy, they have killed me,' and she continued to cry out in pain.

She had suffered 70 per cent burns. In spite of being rushed to hospital, Sudha did not survive. However, the neighbours were not willing to let things go at that and they decided not to let Sudha's in-laws get away. First they chased them to the hospital. They were told that Sudha was being taken to a particular hospital, but when they arrived there, they found she hadn't been brought there. So they searched around in other hospitals in the area and found her at a nearby one. By the time they arrived, Sudha had been forced to give a false statement saying she had been boiling milk and that her clothes had caught fire and she did not want to blame anyone.

Such exonerating statements are very common in the case of dowry deaths. When the woman is burnt and is not in a fit condition to make a statement, the police put stamp pad ink on her thumb and get an impression on a blank sheet of paper which they can then turn into whatever they like. Generally, this is how concocted statements get in. The police do this because, more often than not, the accused buy them over. The only people to lose out in this are the family of the victim. For example, in Hardeep Kaur's case, even though she had given a statement before a magistrate, the police managed to successfully confuse the issue by putting in another statement. Similarly, in Bharati Narula's case too they managed to get another statement which carried her thumb impression on it. It was during the follow-up of her case that the investigating officer proudly explained to me how they managed to get such declarations.

However, Sudha Goel's neighbours were not so easily put off, and they were determined not to allow this fraud to succeed. They gave evidence in court that they had seen Sudha burning while her in-laws simply sat around callously. They also deposed that Sudha's in-laws had tried to prevent them from saving her, and one of them told the judge how he had rushed out to his home and got a blanket to cover Sudha and put the fire out.

As far as I knew, this was the first case in which a death sentence had been given to the accused and it was demoralizing for all of us working on dowry and dowry deaths that the high court acquitted all of them. What was more, in doing so, the judge made a statement that said, 'May be . . . in case she gave birth to a male child they would expect a fridge, or a scooter and cash. It is the custom among Hindus that when the wife delivers, especially a male child, the parents of the girl give gifts to the in-laws.' The judgement showed not only a strong pro-dowry bias but also a strong pro-male prejudice. And as if that was not enough, the judges put in a safety clause to protect themselves saying that if they had erred in their judgement, there was always 'a power above' who was the final arbiter of justice. This, I thought, was a fine escape clause: give a biased judgement and then say that there's always another power that can set this right.

It had all begun innocently enough. I had not been particularly involved in Sudha Goel's case in the initial stages, but since this was a case where capital punishment was awarded, many of us had become interested in it. So when the high court exonerated the accused, we were very unhappy and some of us had gone to the high court to get more information. I was sitting in one of the courtrooms when someone came and whispered that I was wanted outside. 'We're having a meeting, can you come?' I found that a number of women's groups had gathered in the court grounds to protest the judgement. As I walked in someone said, 'Come, Subhadra, we want

you also to support our protest against this judgement.'
I said, 'What judgement, there's nothing but anger . . .'
and had not even got beyond this when a photographer
started clicking away. Later, these photos were submitted
to the high court as proof that women's groups had
intentionally committed contempt of court. Because I
figured in one of the photos, I was among those accused
of contempt. My other companions were Suman Krishan
Kant (wife of the former Vice-President of India) and
Brinda Karat of the All India Democratic Women's
Association. We were all summoned to show cause why
action should not be taken against us for contempt.

My first reaction was of fear: we had been working
with the law, protesting about it, I'd even had a criminal
case slapped on me, but this was something else. How
would I tackle this? This was followed by a kind of
bravado because I thought conviction in this sort of case
would be nothing short of heroic. And then I came down
to earth and realized that there was nothing to be gained
from such heroics, but I also understood that I had to
protect and fight for my right to free expression. I spoke
to the others who had been with us and asked if they
would like to file interventions saying they were all there,
but no one was willing to do this. This again was
disappointing; where, I wondered, was the famed
solidarity among women? When we were called before
the bench, we were asked to go in individually and I
understood that it was a very clever tactic to call each

one separately just to demoralize us.

But I told myself not to worry. I thought, I'm a free citizen of this country and I have a right to express my feelings. Also, it was clear that in this case the judiciary had not been fair in acquitting the accused. So I began to plan how I would appear before the judge and what I would say. Litigation was not a new experience for me. I had earlier fought against my college and won for myself the right to be promoted to a senior grade of Delhi University. I had also joined my family in working hard to evict our tenant who was refusing to leave our hard-earned property, so I was confident that I could stand in the court and hold my own. There were some lawyer friends who offered to take on my case but I had no money and I did not want to take favours from anyone.

I had drafted my own reply and sent seven copies to the court as required. I have never understood why the courts in India do not modernize and make their procedure less cumbersome, but that would probably be too much to expect. Anyway, I prepared myself to appear in court on the appointed day and when I got there I found myself facing two of the most enlightened judges we have, Justice Sachar and Justice Leila Seth. Justice Sachar asked me if I was Brinda Karat. I said no, but secretly I was amused. How could anyone mistake me for such a glamorous, beautiful woman as Brinda? I told myself that perhaps I looked just a teeny bit like her! But then, I rapped myself on the knuckles—figuratively, of course—for such thoughts do not win cases, however pleasing they might be.

I took the initiative and started my rendering by taking a line of offence. I said, 'Your Honours, you are angry and you drag us to court because you say your prestige has been hurt, but when we are hurt by opinions expressed by honourable judges or when you acquit those who are accused in dowry cases and we feel hurt, what can we do except protest? What other way is open to us? What I said at that meeting was only an expression of my feelings of hurt. I did not blame anyone. I simply gave vent to my feeling of resentment which is my fundamental right in a free society. I am confident that you will agree with me in this.'

'Why do you say that?' Justice Sachar asked.

'Look at the number of dowry deaths in the city, and look at the number of acquittals. Should we just keep quiet? And when the trial court finds someone guilty, the high court finds that judgement faulty and acquits the guilty. There is nothing personal in this, but we do feel there should be some kind of deterrent punishment.'

I was quite satisfied with my reply and after the two other co-respondents spoke, the judgement was reserved. Though we had all declared full respect for the country's judiciary and the law, when the judgement was reserved, this served the purpose of punishment, because of the uncertainty that is attached to such decisions. But in 1984, the case had a quiet burial, much to our relief.

Much later, when Justice Sachar retired and was planning to buy a house in Gulmohar Park, he had some problem with the person he was buying from and discussed it with me. He said to me, 'We punished the accused in the Hardeep case because of what you said. Your remarks on dowry were very touching.' I was pleased to hear this of course though I wished the punishment could have been based on the investigation and the facts of the case, which were clear enough.

Convictions and the Benefit of Doubt

I'm often reminded of the Shakespearean quality of mercy when I try to understand the business of the benefit of doubt. For it blesses those who stand on the wrong side of the law and those who deliver the merciful relief. The receiver goes home blessing those who delivered the merciful relief and those who deliver go home to a well-earned rest that they have helped to save another brother from the shackles of law. What does it matter if the woman is left out of this—for that is the normal state of affairs for her anyway. Why else is it that even in the most heinous of cases men are let off on the basis of this ephemeral thing called the benefit of doubt? Here's an example.

Krishna Kumari was a highly educated woman who made her living as a teacher. She was burnt to death in her married home. Her in-laws had demanded a television and a tape recorder. Trouble began to brew as early as the day of the engagement ceremony, but Krishna's father had begged and pleaded with her prospective in-laws and had promised to give them whatever they demanded. As time went on, it became clear that he could not manage this. Krishna brought home a decent salary but this did not put a stop to the demands of her in-laws. She was married in February 1977 and it took a bare few months for her to be burnt to death; she died in April that year. Her burnt body was found lying in the kitchen. It was clear that she had been strangled to death and later set on fire and this was confirmed by the post-mortem report.

The body had obviously been placed in the kitchen and it was speculated that the murderer had escaped through the kitchen window. After the trial the high court ruled that this was a case of homicide and convicted the accused. As often happens, the case then went on appeal to the Supreme Court and it was here that the court, while agreeing fully with the views of the high court, gave the benefit of doubt to the accused and acquitted them.

What could the Court have been thinking of when it brought a judgement of acquittal? Krishna's in-laws were in the house when her death took place. They had pleaded that Krishna had been killed by someone else—but even if someone had managed to sneak into their house and kill their daughter-in-law (which is unlikely), what was his motive? If it was robbery, why was nothing missing from the house? And how is it that he managed to strangle her, drag her body into the kitchen and burn her and then leave? Where was the family? Did they not smell flesh burning? Or hear him dragging her through the house? The case took fourteen years to be decided and perhaps in the eyes of the law this is punishment enough for the accused, but what about justice for the victim? Just because she is no longer there does not mean that she has no right to justice.

Such acquittals encourage crimes because the perpetrator of the crime is convinced that there is a good chance he will get acquitted or that he will just have to spend a few years in jail and can then walk free. This is why men often threaten women saying that while they will manage to be free, the woman will lose her life. Over the years I have realized that acquitted or convicted, it is the man who lives and the woman who dies. Even punishment for life is rarely given: the full term is fourteen years, but judges usually reduce it to seven.

Take the case of Trimbak, who cut his pregnant wife into pieces (in 1996) and hid her head in a bush while the other parts of the body were distributed into two suitcases. He was sentenced to death by the trial court and the high court, but Supreme Court commuted this sentence to life. Apparently what caused the Supreme Court to change the kind of punishment they wanted to give was the fact that the death sentence is given to the rarest of crimes and, according to the judges, dowry deaths are now so common that crimes relating to these do not merit the death sentence. Whether or not you condone the death sentence, you have to admit the illogicality of something like this.

G. Narayan Reddy's daughter was getting engaged to S. Gopal Reddy. The fond father offered to give the prospective bridegroom a house in Hyderabad and Rs 50,000 in cash in addition to expensive clothes and jewellery. But the young Gopal Reddy demanded another Rs 50,000 to buy a car. The father refused and there was an impasse. The father then took the matter to court. The trial court held Gopal Reddy guilty of violation of Section 4 of the Dowry Prohibition Act (DPA). Gopal Reddy then appealed against the judgement to the high court but the high court upheld the lower court's ruling. Finally, the matter went to the Supreme Court. Gopal Reddy argued before the Supreme Court that at the time of betrothal the woman is not a bride so the demands made are not demands made to a bride, and since the young woman was not a bride in the sense described in Section 4, he was not guilty. The Supreme Court did not accept his argument, saying that if his logic was accepted it would defeat the very purpose of the Act. But they gave him the benefit of doubt and acquitted him. The question that comes to my mind here is how does doubt arise in this case? What is it that can lead to giving the accused the benefit of doubt? Gopal Reddy's argument was that of a man who knew what he was doing and in his cleverness he tried to hoodwink the law, and succeeded in doing so.

Gopal Reddy was a trainee for the Indian Administrative Services. I cannot help but believe that it was this, the prospects for his future, that weighed heavily with the judges who gave him the benefit of doubt. In the bargain what they destroyed was the father's faith in the law. A man who had rightfully sought the help of the courts was let down by the fraternal sympathy that pervades the corridors of justice.

Paradoxically, when it comes to dealing with women, the approach is just the opposite. Sometimes judges forget even the basics of courtesy. For instance when Shobha Rani appealed to the court for cancellation of her marriage because her husband was demanding money, the lower and high courts not only rejected her appeal saying that there was nothing wrong in a husband asking for some money from the rich father of his wife but they also dubbed the wife as a sentimental woman who was prone to making a mountain out of a molehill. And they criticized her eating habits. The trial court said there was no demand for anything and, in any case, a demand did not constitute cruelty. I quote from the judgement: 'Though one would not justify demand for money . . . the respondent is a young, upcoming doctor. There is nothing strange in his asking his wife for some money when he needs it . . .' The high court upheld the rejection of the lower court and went a step further in passing derogatory remarks about the wife: 'the petitioner is prone to exaggerate things. This is evident from her complaint of food and the habit of drinking . . . Either because of her oversensitivity, or because of her habit of exaggeration, she has made a mountain out of a molehill.'

The high court added insult to injury by saying that the 'wife seems to be hypersensitive and she imagines too much and too many things'. These remarks were, to my mind, totally uncalled for. Shobha Rani had gone to court trusting that she would get justice and if the judges dealing with her case could not see the genuineness of her demand, they were not justified in going beyond the brief and maligning her in this manner. But then that is the way men treat women, at home, at work and even within the arena of law. Laws are enacted to safeguard the interests of various groups of society and if they are arbitrarily applied without taking into consideration the interests of one section of society they end up doing more harm than good. The judiciary is male dominated and the interests of women find no place in their reckoning. While men use every possible loophole to get their way, the moment women try to do this there is a hue and cry that they are exploiting and misusing the law, and stories of poor suffering husbands or women exploiting the provisions of the anti-dowry law start to circulate. In August 1998, the Times of India Human Rights Watch released stories of such men who had suffered atrocities even though they were 'innocent'. The report said that the law is being used by some vindictive women to squeeze 'the maximum material benefits' and that the person accused by women in such cases is often 'immediately put behind bars and no bail is granted'. I have never heard such nonsense in my life. Interestingly, the report could cite only two cases to prove its point, while for every two such cases there are hundreds which prove exactly the opposite. Despite this, the report says that Section 498A of the law—which allows women to file complaints against men for cruelty, harassment, violence etc.—is violative of the concept of equality and it suggests that a similar law be enacted for men to ensure equality.

On the face of it, such reporting sounds frivolous but it would be a mistake to dismiss it as such. Rather, we need to recognize it as a calculated move to discourage women from fighting for their rights. It is worrying that such thinking is not uncommon and there are many educated people who would subscribe to such views. In 1990, the then Solicitor General of India, Anand Dev Giri, said in a special interview to the *Hindustan Times* that his experience showed him that 'fifty per cent of dowry cases are "vindictive"'. He said he had always defended the accused. One of my friends sent me this clipping, asking me about my reaction to it. I wrote back to my friend that such statements needed to be ignored and that we should continue to fight to have our point of view taken seriously. A woman who is harassed for dowry and then burnt to death cannot be described as vindictive. That people take dowry from women is sufficient proof that women are being victimized, and we need to do something to counter this.

It is because of these kinds of attitudes that the rate of conviction in dowry cases is so low. According to P.K. Dey, an eminent advocate who has fought several such cases, the rate of conviction is barely 3 per cent. There is nothing surprising in this because a dowry death trial is a cumbersome process; it passes through so many hands that anywhere anyone can make a mistake or wilfully do something wrong and the whole trial fails. Generally, mistakes are made because those involved in the investigation do not have any guidelines to fall back upon, but all mistakes are not genuine. The accused knows well that in the whole chain of people involved the policeman can be his best friend and all he has to do is to win him over, by any means, fair or foul.

In any case, even if the trial proceeds systematically and the accused is sentenced to life imprisonment, in most cases he manages to stay out of court by simply not turning up for hearings. In the Sudha Goel case, the accused were convicted but for many years after that they did not go to jail. It was only when the press reported that they were seen walking free that people realized the Supreme Court order had not been implemented. These are not isolated cases. In August 2000, I received a call from a journalist based in the United States about a certain Rajesh Bhalla who, he said, was a runaway convict from India. Bhalla had killed his wife, Renu, and had then used the money he had managed to squeeze from her parents to buy himself a passage to America.

That was in 1983. Seventeen years later, confident that the past was now behind him, he married a divorced woman. It was the divorced husband of this woman who petitioned the courts that Bhalla was a runaway convict from India and asked that his son, who had been taken away by his ex-wife, be protected or given to him.

The journalist who called us wanted to know if there had indeed been a case where Bhalla had been convicted. He asked if we could help him to check this out. Our lawyers went through the court records and we found that the information was correct: Bhalla had been convicted twice, first by the sessions court and then by the high court. He had been sent to jail. A local newspaper in Chandigarh, where the case took place, *The Tribune*, had carried a picture of Bhalla being escorted to jail by the police. Yet this man with a sentence on his head managed to run away from the jail and migrate to the United States and settle down there. When I hear things like this I feel the fight is utterly hopeless.

The Lawmakers and Their Logic

For many years dowry deaths continued to be reported at an alarming rate, almost two a day, with hardly any convictions. In the 1970s when we were active in the campaign against dowry, I remember that Shri Makwana, the then minister for home, informed Parliament that in 1978, thirty cases of dowry deaths had been registered with the police. Of these, only one could be convicted, nine were given the benefit of doubt and the rest were dropped because there was no evidence against them. Three years later the same minister provided different statistics: 390 women burnt to death in 1981 either by 'accident' or 'design'. Of these, only twenty-five cases were filed in court and the others were dropped. He did not mention whether these twenty-five were actually convicted or dropped, a convenient omission.

It is not difficult to understand why convictions are rare in dowry deaths. The crime is committed within the privacy of the home with hardly any witnesses other than those who are a party to it or those who are indifferent and prefer to look the other way. Those who commit the crime are always well prepared with every alibi and excuse in place, and the victim is usually alone and unsuspecting. In most cases, the family of the victim is nowhere near the scene of crime. They are generally not informed in time and often they are out of town and it takes a while for them to reach, by which time all evidence has been destroyed and the woman's body has been cremated or buried. Usually, family members are in shock or emotionally disturbed and cannot give coherent answers when confronted with the intricacies of the law. They make mistakes and these cost them dear for these give enough of a handle to those who apply the law to such situations. For their part, those who plan such murders are aware of this weakness and are therefore confident that they will get away with the crime.

For those who do manage to take cases to court, the prospects are not much brighter. All too often the judicial process fails them, repeated adjournments dampen their faith and, as time passes and the initial shock of grief lessens, the daily routine of life reasserts itself and it begins to seem less and less important to pursue the case. The accused of course know this and bank upon it. In the beginning their attempt is to seek bail. Once this is granted, they know they can get the hearings postponed on one pretext or the other. Either the judge is transferred or an important witness is purchased or reneges and refuses to get involved because of other commitments or the case takes so long that witnesses sometimes die before the hearing takes place.

Often there are inconsistencies in the reports of the judicial or investigating officers, who are not trained to deal with the crime of dowry murders. The government assumes it can treat this crime in the same way it treats others. It has not yet realized the need to train officials to deal with such a crime. Due to these reasons investigating reports are almost always flawed, and because such reports are flawed, the judges often reject them. It is true that there are times when the police slip up because of ignorance—after all, this is a problem they have not been used to dealing with and have no training in how to do so—but most of the time their reports are flawed because they are easily bought over. Families too, understandably, make mistakes in filing reports and once the accused manages to get bail he can do everything possible to ruin the case against him. In the Bharati Narula case, for example, there was just one eyewitness, who turned hostile and refused to testify. No one could understand how or why this had happened. But the explanation is probably a simple one, if we are willing to name it. Apart from the police and the lawyers, the judges are also at fault: when passing judgements they give clear pro-dowry decisions. This is why, even when there is ample evidence of dowry demands and harassment, they tend to give the benefit of doubt to the accused.

Over the years that I have been involved in the campaign against dowry, I have tried to follow dowry cases in the courts but the structure and procedures continue to baffle me. Every judge had a different perception of the crime. Even if some of them believed dowry murder was a major crime, their ways of dealing with it were very subjective and often very anti-woman. The more I saw this the more angry and confused I became. I tried hard to distance myself from the issue and to carry on with my life, but it would not go away.

I thought it might help to discuss it with my lawyer friends—they were many in number. But they were not happy with my constant pestering. They had far too much work of their own to attend to and did not want to be bothered about someone else's agonizing about the rights and wrongs of such an issue. One day, Shyamala Pappu, one of my friends, was so fed up with me that she said, 'Arre baba, why don't you go to the Parliament library and study the making of the law. Then maybe you'll understand that there are so many flaws that it is easy to circumvent it.'

Shyamala was right. After all, it was the legislature which was behind the making of all laws. So it was necessary to go to the source. But visiting Parliament house and using its library was not an easy task. I needed permission from a member of Parliament (MP) who could testify that I was 'a reliable person' and therefore could be allowed access to the library. Once again I went to Shyamala, who directed me to one of our friends and sympathizers in the anti-dowry campaign, Justice

Sunanda Bhandare, whose husband was a member of Parliament. Sunanda helped me get a reference that allowed me to enter the hallowed portals of the Parliament library.

My experience of this library proved very educative. It was a storehouse of information, a virtual goldmine. Spending time there and reading my way through different documents gave me an insight into the thoughts and prejudices of those who make laws and control our lives in this country. I tried to spend as much time as possible there and made frequent visits to the canteen to sustain me through the long hours I was there. Like everything else, I discovered that lawmakers also had subsidized food, unlike us mortals, but at least for those few days I was able to do justice to it. Often, as I ate my way through a subsidized sandwich or cutlet, I would think, 'So many perks and then money, power, importance—all this because we vote them into this position!'

Sometimes on my way to and from the library I ran into a lone MP who seemed to be roaming around aimlessly. On one such occasion I was asked who I was and what I was doing there. I said I was on a research mission, trying to understand the making of the anti-dowry Act. 'Oh that,' said the man, and shrugged and walked away. Obviously dowry is not an important issue for our politicians, even though they made the anti-dowry law. When it came to taking dowry for their sons, most are not in any way recalcitrant, I'm sure. But then it's not really an important issue for anyone, except when it comes to taking money.

Anti-dowry sentiments are not new. In 1978 the National Archives of India held an exhibition on dowry. The report they published as part of this exhibition mentioned that even Akbar had toyed with the idea of doing something against dowry but had refrained from doing so out of political sagacity. In his *Ain-e-Akbari*, he called it a 'mere sham'.

The report also described that in the centuries prior to independence, various attempts had been made at different times to eradicate dowry. During the fifteenth century, the king of Vijaynagar had tried to pass a law against dowry because of reported dowry deaths in his state. There were other such stories as well. But I felt that all these were matters of the past and belonged to a time when India did not have its own government, when it did not exist as a state. My concern was with the anti-dowry measures adopted in independent India.

As I went through the parliamentary debates, I learnt that some MPs of independent India had made a serious attempt to create a law against dowry. In 1953 Uma Nehru, an MP at the time, presented an independent member's bill to ban dowry. But it took the then government almost seven years of constant badgering by women members to finally come out with the Dowry Prohibition Bill. Then it took a further three years of discussion before it became a law.

I went through these discussions in detail. I noticed that the effort, in the discussions, had been not so much to analyse the problem of dowry as it was to support or oppose the ruling party. It's clear from what the MPs said that the stories of young women dying for dowry were not new. As early as 1936 (on 22 February) the *Times of India* had reported that three women had committed suicide by hanging because their father could not meet the dowry demands of their prospective bridegrooms. The three sisters, daughters of a man called K.M. Majumdar, took a joint decision to kill themselves. One of them, Parul, survived and described how the sisters had planned their own deaths. In the family, they were eleven sisters, their only brother was dead and five of the eleven were already married. The same tragedy was repeated in 1996 when once again three young women, sisters, attempted to kill themselves. One survived. Their father had died several years ago and their only brother had a job as a peon. He earned a meagre Rs 2000 a month, an amount which was barely enough to meet the household expenses. He had held off getting married himself for he was keen to get his sisters married first. Several rounds of negotiations with prospective husbands had led to nothing—the stumbling block was always dowry. One day one of the daughters heard her mother and brother discussing this problem. She later told her sisters and they waited for their mother and brother to go to the local temple. While they were away, they took poison in an attempt to kill themselves.

An overheard conversation was also what led Sunita to take her life. She heard her father and maternal uncle talking one day about the difficulty of arranging her marriage because they had no money and the demands were too high. Her father was begging her uncle for some financial support. Sunita was so unhappy and humiliated at this that she burnt herself to death. In her suicide note she specified that the money her father would have arranged for her marriage should be given to her brother. It is not always women who take their lives. So deep is this malaise of dowry that sometimes young men too are driven to despair as was the case with a boy (as reported in the *Times of India* on 27 July 1995) who hanged himself so that his organs could be sold and the money earned from that spent on his sister's wedding.

During the course of the discussions on dowry, many MPs described the plight of young brides who were deserted halfway through the marriage ceremony when bridegrooms, dissatisfied with the dowry, walked out, abandoning the young woman and most probably condemning her to a life spent at the mercy of her relatives. As one MP, A.R. Khan, put it, 'If you take count, you will find that every year the lives of thousands of girls in the country are ruined. If you want to save them you must take steps to control this evil.'

But some others took the opposite stand. They claimed that by trying to ban dowry the government was encroaching on their fundamental rights as guaranteed under Article 19 of the Constitution. 'Who can stop me from giving my daughter what I want? I can do whatever I want with my property.' Unfortunately, the minister of law also took the same view. He referred to the Sarada Act, the prohibiting of child marriages and the Widow Remarriage Act and said that legislation does not help in eradicating social evils—this is something that can only be done through social reform. Even though one might agree with the need for social reform, it was hardly right that a minister of law should profess such little faith in the law. What, then, was he doing in his job?

Jawaharlal Nehru, prime minister at the time, added to this debate when he said, 'Legislation cannot by itself normally solve deep-rooted social problems. One has to approach them in other ways too. But legislation is essential so that it may give that push and have that educative factor as well as the legal sanction behind it which help public opinion to be given a certain shape.'

That was in 1961 when the country was enacting its first legislation on dowry. But today, more than four decades and two amendments later, dowry continues to dog the lives of Indian women, the crime of dowry murder has not been brought under control and no effort has been made to educate people about it. According to Geeta Mukherjee (one-time MP), after the 1984 amendment to the Dowry Prohibition Act, the Tata

Institute in Calcutta conducted an enquiry and interviewed about 600 people. Virtually every single one said he/she had taken/given dowry or would do so. And some 78 per cent of the people spoken to did not even know that there was a law on dowry.

When the Prohibition of Dowry Bill was presented in the Lok Sabha in 1979, there was a great deal of hope and expectation. Those of us who had been agitating against dowry expected the government to enact a legislation that had some teeth and that could go some way towards addressing this ever-increasing problem. But very soon it became clear that such expectations were unrealistic. The trend of discussions and arguments within Parliament made it clear that the entire exercise of getting the government to reconsider the legislation had been more or less futile, and what had been presented in the form of a Bill bore little resemblance to what women's groups had actually demanded.

This disillusionment was not born of any bias against the ruling party—the earlier Bill that had been passed in 1961 had been full of loopholes and contradictions. And from the trend of arguments on the current one, it was clear that the government was not serious about making any changes—perhaps this is why, after it was enacted, the law was just put away on the shelf and no real effort was made to publicize it. Had it been something really new, the government would have lost no time in giving itself public credit for it.

During the course of the discussions the law minister said that social evils such as dowry cannot be eradicated through legislation; rather it was only through education and spreading of awareness that one could hope to eliminate them. Of course this sentiment sounded very good and one could not disagree with it. But we were also aware of the reality that he and his party had done nothing to spread public awareness about dowry. And while he said this because it sounded good, he also pronounced that it was the duty of a father to bedeck his daughter in gold and hand her over to her lord.

Not surprisingly, I thought it inconceivable that the man who subscribed to this way of thinking would be willing to do anything to abolish it. The brochure on dowry which the National Archives brought out traces a long history of efforts to tackle the problem of dowry. Akbar was not the only one who condemned it. There were many others after him who tried to fight it and others, such as Premchand, who wrote about it. In at least two of his novels, *Nirmala* and *Sevasadan*, Premchand describes how the lives of girls are ruined because the parents are unable to give dowry and how they marry them off to unsuitable partners. Indeed, dowry was also a concern of many of the people involved in the nationalist movement and both Gandhi and the Arya Samaj spoke out against it.

In the late 1970s women's groups began to agitate for changes in the existing law on dowry. Over the years, each time they had tried to take a case of dowry harassment or death to the courts, they were faced with an insipid law. The government at the time responded to the demands of women's groups and appointed a special committee of both houses of Parliament, a joint select committee, to look into the existing law and to suggest amendments and additions. The committee was advised to produce its report quickly because of the urgency of the situation—instances of dowry death were on the rise and it was clear that the existing law was unequal to addressing the problem.

The select committee travelled all over India and invited people such as lawyers, activists, teachers and social workers to speak to them. They also circulated a questionnaire asking for advice and clarifications and they made full use of the media. Their travels were widely publicized and people came and offered to speak to them. I was also invited to speak before the committee. I was quite nervous at the prospect of having to appear before a government body because I did not know how they would react to my very strong views on dowry. Somewhat hesitantly, I presented myself at Parliament house on the appointed day and was escorted to the committee room. Somehow this little consideration made me feel more confident and relaxed than I had earlier done.

Once inside, I felt more at ease because I had worked as an activist with some of the members of the committee. When I said that to my mind dowry was a slight to the dignity of women, Mrs Krishna Sahi, the chairperson of the committee, expressed her disagreement with me. 'Do you mean to say dowry should be abolished?' she asked me. 'Yes,' I said.

'Do you mean we should send our daughters to their matrimonial homes like beggars?'

I was somewhat shaken by this approach of the chairperson—how could a committee chaired by someone who felt like this recommend any improvements to the existing Act? But I was younger at the time and had the confidence of my convictions. I looked at all the VIPs gathered in the room and said to them, 'I brought no dowry with me when I married. Do I look like a beggar to you?' There was a ripple of embarrassed laughter, but I was glad I had had the courage to say what I felt. The committee questioned me further and now I was able to reply with confidence and assert what I felt.

My experience at this interview made me optimistic. When I look back on it now I feel that I was not only young at the time but also quite innocent. I felt the members had been responsive and that they had done a lot of work in reaching out to people and soliciting their views. So I looked forward to the day when the findings of the committee would be made public and implemented by the government. But to my disappointment, the government sat over the report after having initiated the work of the committee and it was only in 1982, when considerable pressure was mounted by women's groups, that the government tabled the report and a year later the new law came into force.

The committee had made seventeen recommendations for changes. The government ignored all but three of them. Then people began to ask why they had constituted the committee in the first place: why spend so much time and money only to ignore the very important suggestions the committee had made on the basis of its discussions with activist groups. For example, one of the things women's groups had asked for was the institution of dowry prohibition officers, special officers who would be trained to investigate dowry cases and submit their reports. But no such officers were appointed. On another aspect the committee and the Law Commission had both recommended changing the definition of dowry—as it existed, it was vague and unclear. The new definition suggested by the Law Commission was very comprehensive: dowry, it said, was, 'Dowry, or other things estimable in terms of money relatable only to the wife's having married into the husband's family.' But the government ignored all these suggestions and amended the existing definition merely by replacing 'in consideration' with 'in connection with marriage'. The matter was further complicated when, in addition to the definition and explanation, were added gifts which were customary and 'in keeping with the status of the family'. In other words, according to the law, the giving of such gifts did not amount to dowry.

One of the things activists had demanded was that the law lay down some guidelines for austerity in marriages. This was not a new demand. Social organizations had long emphasized the need for simple marriages. In the earlier forms of Hindu marriage at least, ceremonies had been performed in the open, under the stars, for this was supposed to be auspicious. Now, with the emphasis on exhibiting one's riches, venues began to shift to five-star hotels and everywhere people tried to outdo each other in lavish displays of wealth. People attending marriages would be covered in jewellery; the bride and bridegroom's families would leave no stone unturned to show off how much they had spent or were giving away; enormous mountains of food would be cooked and much of it wasted, not to mention the excessive use and wastage of electricity and water. As a result of this, what should be a happy occasion often turns into something ugly, leaving a bad taste in the mouth. I remember when my sister's daughter was getting married, the prospective in-laws insisted that they be allowed to bring 1100 guests because they were from a well-known business community and it was impossible for them to leave anybody out. For my sister, this became a terrible strain: where was she to find the money to feed 1100 people, and, indeed, where would there be a space large enough to house them? After much discussion—a lot of it unpleasant—back and forth, the number was reduced to 400. Clearly the marriage was not meant for the couple who were marrying—no one had thought to ask them what they wanted—but it was an excuse to oblige friends and colleagues!

What made it worse was that in the end only eighty people came. So, huge amounts of money and food were wasted. When my sister tried to ask why the number had been so reduced, she was told this was the privilege of the in-laws, of the boy's family. Since this wedding was in the middle of summer, there was little we could do to preserve the food. So my sister's husband spent the next few days distributing food. At the end of this he was exhausted and both he and his wife felt cheated by their daughter's in-laws—not a good way to start a new relationship. The marriage did not last beyond two years.

Often people don't think at all about the grossness and inappropriateness of such ostentation. Who knows whether or not a marriage will last? There are two instances related to this which stick in my mind. One was the marriage of the daughter of a minister in Delhi. Virtually all rooms in a five-star hotel in the city were booked, people were flown in from all corners of the globe, designers were commissioned to decorate the marriage pandal and others to dress the bride and bridegroom and chefs were flown in to cook gourmet meals. But within two years, the marriage ended in the bitterest of divorces. Similarly, in 1962 we were invited to attend the marriage of a relative. The list of dinner guests was three-tier. At the top were the VIPs who were treated to the best food and were even served champagne. Then came the second tier of important friends and close family and we were in the third tier of ordinary people. The marriage decorations were remarkable: I remember noticing that banana tree stumps had been hollowed out and lights shone from inside them. Everything looked outstanding—it was clearly a marriage of the rich for the rich. But no one seemed to have bothered to ask the bride what she wanted. It clearly wasn't this marriage for, a short while later, she killed herself, apparently suffocated by the wealth of the family. All too often, this is the plight of many young women who enter their married homes with such hopes and dreams. But for those who negotiate and arrange such marriages, these are the only times they can show off their wealth and dispose of their ill-gotten gains (for most of the money spent on such occasions is black money).

But often, I found, that people did not even want to speak about black money. For example, when the anti-dowry agitation was at its height in Delhi, Meera Dewan, a film-maker, made a film on dowry which she called *Gift of Love*. She was keen to interview me for the film. But when I began to talk about black money, she got worried and asked me not to do so. Her argument was that her film was funded by the government and she did not want to incorporate anything that might prove problematic. I refused to change anything I had said, but sadly, she exercised her editorial privilege and deleted my statements from the film. I wondered, if we are so scared to speak about black money, how will we ever address the problem of dowry?

In 1976 Sanjay Gandhi, Indira Gandhi's infamous son, introduced a guest control order in Delhi: only a certain number of guests could be invited to attend weddings. People grumbled and complained. But they were not the ones whose lives were being sacrificed to keep up the image of wealth for their families. Surprisingly, in no instance are young women consulted about whether or not they want such lavish expenditure on their marriages. It is quite possible that many of them may prefer to cut down on such expenditure and use the money better elsewhere. Sanjay Gandhi's guest control order however was promulgated during the state of emergency in the country, so no one dared protest about it and it had to be implemented. I remember that weddings during this period became pleasurable because they were so simple and no one felt the strain of having to spend huge amounts of money or to give expensive gifts or to dress up in jewels and rich silks. But the reprieve was short-lived. Sanjay Gandhi was killed in a flying accident, and the order promulgated by him lapsed by default. In 1991 the Chandrashekhar government tried to bring it in again, announcing that as part of its austerity measures a guest control of a maximum of 100 guests would be kept on marriages and parties. But this time round there was such strong protest that the order had to be withdrawn. The government tried to save face by saying that it would soon announce a new date for bringing in the order but this never happened.

It was rumoured that the prime minister's office was put under a great deal of pressure from some business people to withdraw the order. Clearly the kind of pressure the business community can exercise is of a different nature from that of the activists, for seldom, if ever, has the government been known to give in to this latter kind of pressure. For example, when the Asha Rani case was being argued, the judge had said that the government should adopt a policy to see that those men who kill their wives for dowry should not be allowed to marry again, as otherwise they will make a business out of murder and marriage. Earlier several women's groups had suggested something similar and had also asked for compulsory registration of marriages. Similarly, when the Dowry Prohibition Act of 1961 was being debated, an MP, Mr Hem Baruah, had said in Parliament that by way of educating people a very small but significant step that could be taken was for the government to declare the giving or taking of dowry illegal. A similar proposal had been made by the joint committee of Parliament when it submitted its report in 1982. At that time, residents of Gulmohar Park who protested the death of Bharati Narula had submitted a memorandum to the prime minister, Indira Gandhi, saying that newspapers should carry a 'warning' alongside matrimonial advertisements that dowry is an offence in law just as there is a statutory warning which is published alongside cigarette ads, etc. Unfortunately, when activists and other concerned persons agitate against dowry and seek the cooperation of the government, they get no response. But when heavyweight businessmen put pressure on the government, it takes no time at all for the government to cave in to their demands. This indifference is the main reason why people even in important public offices get away with dowry offences.

Prejudice and Bias

Although several years have passed since the Tata Institute's survey in Calcutta, I have no doubt that knowledge about the existence of a law on dowry has not greatly improved. If ordinary people do not know about such a law, there is perhaps some excuse that can be found for this—it is, after all, the responsibility of the state to ensure that its citizens are aware of the laws that govern their lives, just as much as it is the responsibility of the citizens to find out about such laws. But the same excuse cannot apply to those who make and provide laws. Judges, in particular, are expected to know the law they dispense and to understand the spirit in which it was made. It is possible they may be quite familiar with the law. But that is not all that governs their judgements, for there is also the small matter of their approach and how understanding and flexible it is of realities on the ground. Much of the time, this all-important flexibility is lacking, and often during the trial they make very biased statements against women. In 1981, a judge actually delivered a judgement in a dowry case (Inder Sain *vs* the State) in which he said (according to the *Times of India*) that anything given after the marriage did not count as dowry. In another case (Vinod Kumar *vs* the State of Punjab) the judge said that the very concept of a matrimonial home connotes 'jointness' of possession and custody by the spouses. In the Shobha Rani *vs* Madhukar Reddy case, Shobha Rani asked for divorce from her husband for demanding dowry and she produced a letter, as evidence, which was written by her husband justifying his parents asking for dowry. It said, 'Now regarding the dowry point I still feel there is nothing wrong in my parents asking for a few thousand rupees. It is quite a common thing for which my parents are being blamed as harassment.'

In themselves, many of these statements about joint possessions or custody or one spouse asking the other for money may not be particularly objectionable. But it is when they are seen in the context of dowry demands and harassment, violence against the wife, often leading to her death, that they acquire a sinister significance and should be seen as such. In the above case, fortunately, the Supreme Court understood the wife's contention and held the husband guilty of marital offence. The judge stated quite clearly that 'judges and lawyers should not import their own values of life'. He went on to say that there may be a generation gap between judges and the parties on whom they were pronouncing judgement. It would therefore be better if the judges kept aside their own customs and manners and 'if they depended less on precedents'. Meaning thereby that judges should not bring their private prejudices and beliefs into the judgements they make, a particularly important thing to keep in mind.

The high court made a similar observation in another case. Chanda was burnt to death within five days of her marriage. There was ample evidence against the in-laws who had been dissatisfied because the dowry was not enough for them. At the marriage they had expressed their unhappiness with the amount of money she had brought. Later, when her brother came to visit her, they did not allow him to meet with her. In her dying declaration, Chanda implicated her husband and the police report showed that the husband was seen coming down the stairs calmly while his wife was burning. Despite this the high court acquitted the husband saying, 'It all depends on the reaction of the individual . . . whether he attempts to save at the risk to his life . . . this by no stretch of imagination can prove that he committed the crime.' Luckily, in this case too this judgement was struck down by the Supreme Court where the judge said, 'the court must display greater sensitivity to criminality . . . and avoid soft justice.'

But such sage advice is seldom followed and instances where courts display the kind of sensitivity that such cases need are rare. More often than not, judges overlook the concept and spirit of the anti-dowry legislation and make observations which are very damaging to women.

As if all this were not worrying enough, as I read through judgements, I came across even worse instances of discrimination and bias. In another case (Jagdish Chander *vs* State of Haryana) the woman, Savitri Devi, died of burns in her husband's house. There were various reasons why charges could not be framed against the husband, one of them being the delay in filing the case. But the judge dealing with the case said, 'wilful conduct of the accused in taking liquor daily despite constant protests by his wife and his habit of coming home late at night does not fulfil the essential ingredients of cruelty . . . the husband cannot be made responsible for the suicide of a sentimental woman who did not like the drinking habits of her husband.'

I wondered if the judge did not find alcoholism and wife-beating objectionable because that is the way marriages are run in our country. Hence a woman goes to court with a complaint against her husband and the high court is shocked. How dare she do this? Better for the law not to interfere with the sanctity of marriage. And if the woman dies in the bargain, well that has to be her fault. As one judge said in another case (H. Singh *vs* H. Singh), 'the introduction of law in the home is like introducing a bull in a china shop . . . it will be a ruthless destroyer.' Does it ever occur to judges to ask if the sanctity of the home can be preserved or should be preserved at the cost of the woman's dignity, her human rights and her life? But this is not the way they are trained to think or believe. Why then should we blame lesser mortals when those who dispense justice are themselves flawed? Even the Chief Justice of India in 1990, Ranganath Misra, thought nothing of saying in a seminar that 'women should go back to their homes . . . God has not created man and woman as equal . . .' If this is how the Chief Justice of the country thinks, there is little we can hope for. The sad part of something like this is that no one can censure the Chief Justice. Later, at some point he did offer a mild apology, but by that time the damage had been done.

It is clear to me that all the men in the profession have the same approach: to keep women in bonds. But sometimes I feel that parents who grieve after the death of a daughter are no less to blame. Their sorrow comes only when they are faced with the reality of their daughter's death. Asha Rani, whose father was unable to pay even as small an amount as Rs 5000, was beaten up several times and her father had to live with this knowledge. He had seven daughters to marry off and if the marriage of one of them was broken, it would affect the prospects of all the others.

I remember reading about an unfortunate young woman who was working in Delhi as a librarian. After she was married she went to Bihar where her married home was. Soon she was faced with continuing demands for more dowry or money. She wrote to her father saying she would like to come home, but her tradition-bound father wrote back that the only solution was for her to learn to adjust. And then, ostensibly to help his daughter, he sent her letter and his reply to her father-in-law who was of course furious. Consequently she did not have a quiet moment in the house. Once again she tried to reach her father, this time from her uncle's home in Allahabad. The father refused to listen to her plea and told her she must go back to her husband. This she eventually did and was never heard of again.

Recently, there was another disturbing incident. A young girl walked into my office. She was bleeding from the head. When I asked what had happened, she explained that her alcoholic husband had hit her on the head with a bottle. We took her to the police and registered a case. But then, she suddenly backed out. The police officer told her that if she went back to her husband, she would not come away alive. But she said there was no way she could go back to her parents and she did not have anywhere else to go so she went back. This was not the first time her husband had attacked her: earlier he had stabbed her in the arm when he was drunk. But I kept thinking that if she had gone to her parents' house or if they had been willing to take her back she could at least have led a life of dignity as a person on whose marriage they had spent their life's earnings. But there are so many ifs that you can ask these questions endlessly.

The Importance of Resistance

As we came across more and more anti-woman judgements we thought that we should try to introduce some kind of sensitivity among judges so that they could begin to understand what women were going through. During this period we were working with Justice P.N. Bhagwati, the then Chief Justice of India. We were working on the projects of setting up a para legal brigade and providing free legal aid. During the course of our discussions with him I brought up the suggestion of accountability of judges, with a view to creating sensitivity, and I referred to various observations that different judges had made in the cases we were familiar with. The Chief Justice was not very responsive to the idea but he did not object to our going ahead. So we tried to send a feeler to him through a friend, who told us that he was willing to meet us. We were excited, hoping that something would come of the meeting. But it seems that at the last moment he developed cold feet and he backed out of the prospect of meeting 'so many angry women'. We were disappointed as there were many things we wanted discussed and clarified.

However, we were quite amused when the same judge sent us a message after a few days that one of his very close relatives who was married in Chandni Chowk was in difficulty in her married home and asked if we could look her up and inform him. We were quite disappointed with the judge for letting us down but we decided to look up the woman in the hope that this might help in opening a dialogue with him. If we are able to get him to take us seriously, we thought, it might be one way of beginning a dialogue.

I did not want to go alone because I was not familiar with the area, so I asked a friend of mine, C.B. Muthamma (whom we called Muthu), a retired Indian foreign service officer, to accompany us. As Muthu and I walked into the narrow sunless lanes of Chandni Chowk we felt we were out on a dangerous trek. The streets were full of slush and we had to pull our saris up to keep them dry, but we could not save our shoes or our feet. The address was also very complicated and we had to keep asking people for directions. Finally, when we reached the place we found that the family lived on the third floor and there were a lot of stairs to climb. But we had to go since we had committed ourselves to doing so. For Muthu it was more of an ordeal since she had most recently been a VIP, but we laughed and went on.

The house was a sort of open space with rooms all round. At one end was something that resembled an improvised kitchen. We had not yet knocked when a rather fat woman emerged from the opposite side. Without so much as a glance at us, she pulled up her sari and sat down and piddled on one side of the kitchen. Then she called a young child and said, 'You also do it and I will pour water and wash it away.' Accordingly, the kid also did it.

Muthu and I looked at each other a bit bewildered and amused and the same thought crossed both our minds—that before things go any further we must knock. So we did, loudly. The woman looked at us and asked us what we wanted. We did not want to tell her why we had come so we lied, 'We're doing some research in this area and we want to know if you have any girls in the house—your daughter or a daughter-in-law.' She called her daughter. The girl looked very well dressed, she wore bright lipstick, a mini skirt, high-heeled shoes . . . the works. While we were talking to her, the daughter-in-law emerged. We thought she was the maid. But the daughter introduced her as her sister-in-law, saying that she wasn't fond of wearing nice clothes and, in any case, 'Her parents did not give her much to be proud of.'

We asked if we could speak to her. She said yes, and went downstairs. In that brief moment we told the young woman who we were and why we had come. She was quite miserable but she did not want us to tell her parents. 'They'll be unhappy,' she said. 'You see, we are banias and banias are very orthodox. We would rather let our girls die in their matrimonial homes than allow them to complain or go back home. There is a lot of social humiliation and indignity if we do.'

She told us that her in-laws had taken away all her jewellery, they'd given her saris away at weddings and she was made to do all the hard work and slog at home. In addition, she had to listen to taunts all the time about not having brought enough dowry with her. We asked about her husband. She said he did not say anything and usually kept silent when her mother-in-law taunted and tortured her. This was enough for us to understand the situation. She was alone and no one was willing to help her.

We brought this information back to the judge but for some reason he seemed to have lost interest in the young woman and her plight and he was not at all responsive. He said that if she did not want to raise the subject with her parents, we should just leave it, and in the end that was what we had to do. This sort of indifference was something we came across repeatedly, but much of the time people simply ignored the fate of the daughter or sister they had given away in marriage. In this case, what intrigued us was that he had asked us to go and check out the situation, but when we did he did not seem to be interested in taking things any further. Without his nod we could not go ahead with any kind of intervention, the more so when the woman herself did not want us to do so. This is another terrible bind: women who are victims of dowry violence are adults, and in theory they should be capable of making their own choices. In actual practice the 'choice' they make is not really a choice at all, and is something they have been conditioned into believing is right, even if it goes against their own interest. For the women's group wishing to intervene, then, things become quite complicated: whose wishes and beliefs do you go by? And what do you do when the two contradict each other? There are no easy answers to this—for the most part you can only hope that the woman herself wants and needs the support of the women's group.

But not everyone is as indifferent as this judge, and it is this occasional example of something positive—an initiative taken by someone or resistance to unjust marriages on the part of women—that helps to keep our courage and faith. Without these, it would have been extremely difficult to carry on. I remember one such instance took place in 1987 when a group of academics, journalists and activists presented a memorandum to the home minister (of state), P. Chidambaram. They reported that they had been to the Lal Bahadur Shastri Academy in Mussoorie to speak with probationers and officers of the Indian Administrative Services (IAS). Government officers and those starting their careers in government service are given training in the form of short and long courses at the academy. During the training, visiting academics and experts give lectures on a range of subjects. At the time, in 1987, a group of people (including me) who had gone to speak to junior officers on issues of gender (and specifically dowry) were shocked to find that the majority of them had no compunctions at all about taking dowry (most of them were male). The letter to the minister said:

> During our visit to the Lal Bahadur Shastri National Academy of Administration at Mussoorie, we were shocked to learn that the majority of the probationers who get married after joining the service, openly take dowry, negotiated by themselves or, with their knowledge and consent, by their parents. The amounts involved are usually staggering. We understand that some have received up to Rs 30–35 lakhs, with recent promises even extending to Rs one crore, while Rs 15–20 lakhs are said to be commonplace. The sums vary by the probationer's caste, community and state of origin and are pushed up further by the state of allotment [i.e. the area/state to which the person is sent to to work]. The rates are openly discussed among the probationers without the slightest shame or hesitation—indeed, with pride—regardless of the fact that the taking of dowry is a specific offence under the Dowry Prohibition Act, as well as under the conduct of rules of the All India and Central Services. They set the pace too for the escalation of dowry all over the country.
>
> Also, the practice is corrupting our entire body politic. That the same probationer can command

different amounts depending on his state of allotment no doubt relates, among other things, to the varying opportunities for extra-legal earnings in different states. In the process, the girl's parents also appear to be seeking to purchase, through their sons-in-law, government help and protection for strengthening their own economic and political positions.

Indeed, downstream corruption is inherent in this process. A man who has taken what amounts to a bribe for future favours to his in-laws, and committed a criminal offence at the outset of his career, can hardly be expected to subsequently maintain the high standards of integrity expected of him, leave alone implement anti-dowry and anti-corruption laws, or work towards improving the status of women in India. That such officers will be our future policy makers, planners and administrators is a matter of gravest concern to all of us.

It is imperative, therefore, that the Government take serious note of this problem, institute an enquiry into its spread and initiate immediate steps to eliminate it. A start could be made by enforcing existing provisions in the laws, supplemented by appropriate stringent administrative actions. It may also be mentioned here that the Director of the Academy has a specific duty under Rule 3(2) (I) of the Conduct Rules to 'ensure the integrity and devotion to duty of all Government servants for the time being under his control and authority.'

We would, therefore, like to suggest the following measures for consideration:

1. All probationers who are unmarried when joining the service be asked to declare in writing, at the time of joining that neither they nor anyone on their behalf, will take or give dowry. This declaration be placed in their service records, and failure to make such a declaration be treated as behaviour unbecoming of a government servant and disciplinary action initiated accordingly.

2. All IAS probationers already married at the time of joining the service be asked to declare in writing that neither they nor anyone else on their behalf, has taken or given dowry during or after their weddings. Failure to give such a declaration be treated as admission after the fact and action taken accordingly.

3. The personnel department take responsibility for verifying, from time to time, that the declarations have not been violated, receive complaints against any violations, and start investigations against those officers who are known to have taken dowry at the time of their weddings, or at any time thereafter.

4. A letter be addressed by the Director of the Academy to all parents of probationers specifying that their children would be liable to disciplinary action, and even prosecution, if it is found that there has been a negotiation, demand or acceptance of dowry at the time of their weddings, or any time thereafter.

5. The Government seriously consider the

implications of allotting any probationers their home states which, among other things, appears to materially affect the rates of dowry.

6. The probationers, on joining the Academy, be sensitized and made fully aware of the wider and serious social implications of the issue.

Similar measures would be needed for other All India and Central Services, as well as the State Civil Services.

By a combined strategy of the sort developed above, we do believe that some start can be made towards curbing the practice and, over time, gradually isolating and weeding out those who persist.

The minister assured the group who met him that he would see what remedial steps could be taken while the probationers were still undergoing training at the academy. But of course nothing was done. Later a national newspaper, *The Indian Express*, even suggested that punitive action such as dismissal be taken against the offending officers as taking dowry amounted to a blatant violation of the law of the land, but this suggestion too went unheeded. Nonetheless, we took heart from the fact that at least the visitors to Mussoorie had felt concerned enough to protest about what was happening.

While I was still teaching at Dayal Singh College I

often visited the Cottage Industries Emporium at Janpath, the well-known shopping centre. I often found the quiet elegance of Cottage, as it used to be known, quite refreshing and as I walked up and down the stairs I would forget the tensions of life and come home feeling better—and of course with my purse much lighter. I also liked to eat at Bankura, a small eating place next to Cottage. I liked the food and the atmosphere and the fact that it was run by a group of women.

One day as I sat there eating a delicious lunch, I spotted a familiar face smiling at me. I recognized Subhash, my friend from college, but wondered what she was doing here in Delhi without her husband. She had married only a year or so ago. And yet, I thought, if something serious had happened, she would not have been here looking so happy. So I walked up to her and said, 'What are you doing here? I thought you were in Srinagar?'

'Not any longer,' she said with a sad smile. 'I'm working in Delhi now.'

'Working?' I said, with some surprise. 'Working here?' But why, I wondered, what's happened to the husband? She sensed my thoughts and said, 'Yes, I have left him.'

'But what happened?' I asked her.

Apparently, Subhash's sister had come to spend her holidays with the new couple and soon her sister and husband developed a relationship. 'I think I had too much confidence in our relationship,' she told me. 'I was too naive and trusting and I did not really notice what was going on. When my sister's holidays came to an end and I asked her what her plans were for returning, she told me, "I think now it is you who must go and leave us to ourselves." I could not believe this. I was furious, I screamed and shouted but what was the use? Then I wrote to my father and asked him to help resolve the problem. Instead, he wrote back and suggested I go back to him. He said, "Why do you want to stick around with a man who is not worth trusting? Come back and I will find you another man and the big dowry I had set aside for your sister can go with you."

'My father's attitude made me even more angry. Is dowry all that marriage is about? What about my right to happiness? Are material goods all that a woman wants? And most of all, is that the only duty parents have towards their children? The only thing that I felt grateful for was the education that my parents had given me. Of course I found it difficult to cope. I would weep all the time in my loneliness. But then, one morning I made up my mind to leave and look for a job elsewhere. I began to scan the advertisements and to send in applications and finally I got called for an interview. I rushed to Delhi without informing anyone. I think I had some crazy idea that if I did not find a job I would kill myself. But I got the job and here I am, happy and independent.'

I asked Subhash whether she did not feel bitter and

resentful towards her family. She said yes, she did, especially as it was her own sister who had done this to her. But then, she had also asked herself, why blame only her sister, why not the man as well? By and large, though, she felt comfortable and happy. She laughed as she said this and her laughter was infectious. I found myself laughing as well and rejoicing with her for her independence and confidence.

On my way home I thought a lot about Subhash and I felt a sense of quiet happiness that there was some hope somewhere, that there were women who could, even in the worst of situations, take sensible decisions about their lives. And Subhash wasn't alone in this. In Karmika, we had dealt with a few cases where women had made their own private rebellions. I remember the case of Neetu, the daughter of a rich businessman, who had been married into an equally rich home but the marriage had brought her no happiness. After her father died, Neetu's mother found her daughter too much to handle, she felt she was getting out of hand, so she married her off. In her married home, Neetu was faced with a stern, orthodox mother-in-law who made her do all the household work, saying that in their household it was the duty of the daughter-in-law to look after everyone. Neetu's husband clearly concurred in this for he did not do or say anything to help her.

One day Neetu decided to walk out. She came to us and asked if we could find her a temporary shelter and we sent her to a short-stay home. Such institutional support is absolutely crucial for women to have the confidence to take decisions. Neetu's father-in-law and husband found out that we had helped her and they threatened to report us to the police for having 'enticed her away'. But we were secure in the knowledge that Neetu was safe and since she is an adult we could not be held responsible for her decisions. Shortly after this, Neetu's mother asked her to come home, promising to respect her wishes and Neetu went. We helped her to get her dowry back from her husband and soon she filed for divorce. Once the divorce came through she lived on her own until she met someone else and married him and ultimately found happiness.

Most of the time parents and others are guilty of denying women any role. They think women are unintelligent, that they are incapable of taking decisions and therefore they do not even try to involve them in decisions. And yet, if they would just stop to think, they'd find that given the opportunity women are perfectly capable of making their own intelligent decisions.

There was a young woman called Sarbat Kaur who was all ready to leave with her husband after her marriage ceremony when suddenly he began to make demands. He was obviously exploiting the fact that the marriage was now a fait accompli and this was the moment when he could put pressure and expect his demands to be met. But he had reckoned without Sarbat Kaur, his bride.

The moment she became aware of what was going on, she pulled off her wedding bangles and threw them at her husband, saying that she refused to spend her life with a man like him. Her actions created a furore and the police came in and registered a case of dowry harassment and took the husband and father-in-law into custody.

Similarly, another young woman called Neelam refused to marry the man she was engaged to. When she heard that he was demanding dowry—he had asked for Rs 50,000, a scooter and some gold—she just picked up the phone and told the prospective bridegroom that he need not bother to come, she wasn't going to marry anyone like him. At the time, Neelam's father was not alive and she was dependent on her brothers, yet she had the courage to tell this man she would not marry him and condone his greed. Neelam's mother was unhappy as she felt her daughter's actions would bring humiliation to the family. But that did not happen. Instead, a large number of people from the neighbourhood came to congratulate the family for their daughter's courage. This just shows how much people are against the custom of dowry even though they do not have the courage to fight.

In the 1950s when I was in Ambala I'd heard of a similar incident. A young bride had walked out of her marriage ceremony protesting against the greed of the bridegroom and his demands. The bridegroom later insisted he wanted to marry the same woman because he admired her courage, but she refused. At that time I did not attach any importance to this incident but today I am filled with admiration for this young woman and I wish we had thousands more like her.

Unfortunately, that is not the case, but these incidents at least show that there are women who can and do resist, and they are ordinary women like anyone else.

Bringing Things to a Close

We have been told all our lives that dowry is a gift, given at the time of marriage when the kanya or virgin is given away, usually by her father. Along with the gift of a virgin, we were told, there had to be another gift, because according to the rules laid down by our religious gurus, the gift of a virgin must be accompanied by a 'dakshina' or a voluntary donation. During the debates on the Dowry Prevention Act in 1959, when the Bill to prohibit dowry was being discussed, one of the members of Parliament clarified that even if it was one rupee that was being given, no marriage could be considered a marriage if there is no 'dakshina'. And yet, I have often wondered how we can call something a gift which brings such violence and sorrow into women's lives.

As a custom, dowry is said to have been prevalent among the rich and propertied classes. Apparently, it was believed that women were not competent to handle property and so at the time of marriage, when the daughter was virtually leaving home for good, she was given dowry to compensate for what she would lose out in terms of the family fortune. Apart from this logic, the rich also used the giving and taking of dowry to cement ties with other rich families and also managed to keep the son-in-law at a distance from their family property for no one wanted him to be given the chance to touch this wealth.

Among the not so rich, the custom of bride price—almost the opposite of dowry—prevailed. Here, the prospective groom had to pay a price to take away the bride. It is believed that as poorer sections of society began to aspire to move up in the social scale, they emulated the practice of dowry which came to be seen as markers of status. In addition, political uncertainties meant that parents were increasingly unsure about the welfare of their daughters and began to woo prospective grooms with offers of dowry. Once rising unemployment and rampant consumerism were added to this, the resulting mixture was a potent one, with people beginning to see dowry as a quick path to satisfying their greed for goods and money.

Superstition and myth added to this: Hindus believe that it is the moral duty of a father to bedeck his daughter with gold and hand her over to her 'lord'. Since marriage is the only sacrament allowed to women, it was essential that daughters be married off, else they would not go to heaven and would turn into ghosts. There is a well-known story that illustrates this: Shuru, the daughter of sage Kuni, refused to marry despite her father's efforts to make her do so. Apparently, when she was about to die, she was told she could not go to heaven as her body had not been purified by the sacrament of marriage. Thereafter, a hasty marriage was conducted before she breathed her last.

How can we get rid of this blatant insult and exploitation of women, especially when most people are totally convinced that dowry is their right? I remember that one of the many times that I was fired with enthusiasm to do something about dowry, I drafted a letter to the government asking for a thorough change in the law relating to dowry. I shared this with my colleagues in the college where I taught and asked if they would be willing to sign it. One of them got into quite a debate with me. 'Why should I not take dowry?' he asked. 'I will have to provide for the woman for the rest of my life. She'll eat in my home, at my expense. The least her parents can do is provide for her food.' I was really taken aback. I had never been faced with such commercialization of marriage. And this from a teacher! What must he be teaching to his students? As we were arguing, another colleague walked in and asked what was going on and he was told, 'This madam here is asking me to sign a letter protesting against dowry. How can I do that? Dowry is part of our rich heritage and it is a custom that has been followed for so long. Mercifully we have not yet given up our culture even though we have imbibed so much foreign culture.' Such opinions are common, and my colleagues were not alone in their beliefs. My own sister had refused to get her son married if his in-laws did not provide a motorcycle in their daughter's dowry.

*

As I write these words I am only a few days away from my eightieth birthday. For more than a quarter century I have been involved in the anti-dowry agitation. Even though I had never been a supporter of dowry, I can't say that I opposed it in any active way until the death of Hardeep Kaur, a tragic circumstance which catapulted me into the thick of agitation. The vision of that young woman, wrapped in a white sheet so that her burns would not be visible, is still fresh in my mind and often haunts me. What must she have felt as she watched her husband and mother-in-law set fire to her? I continue to be troubled by this. What have we done, I often ask myself, to ensure that the world is a better place for young women to grow up and live in?

In the course of my work on dowry I have come across every sort of corruption: the courts, the law, the systems of justice, police investigations, political interference, not to mention the corruption of custom and tradition. The people who seem to matter least in this are women. There have been times when I have felt enormously tired, when I have despaired because nothing ever seems to change, yet every time I have been accosted by such a feeling something has happened—a small victory, a woman who has resisted—to make me feel better. I think the ups and downs will continue as long as I am able to continue this work, which, given my age, I don't think will be much longer. Of course one benefit of age is that people think white hair is inevitably accompanied by a fund of knowledge, and therefore they are only too willing to trust you and work with you.

But now that I look back on my years of work and my development as a human being, I realize that there were many lessons that I picked up along the way. A small incident from my school years sticks in my mind. As a child I wanted to attend parties all the time and once I wanted to wear lipstick to a friend's birthday. My mother did not allow me to do so, saying, 'Not here. When you go to your own home you can do anything.' I was stunned—I looked at my mother in disbelief. I was close to tears and my mother must have seen this for she put her arms around me and tried to explain. But I refused to listen. I thought, I was born here, I have grown up here, how can she disown me like this? If I don't belong here, then where do I belong?

But several years into my marriage I began to believe that there was some truth in what she had said to me. As my family grew I became more and more involved in the daily preoccupations of my home and the memory of that hurt began to fade. In my new home there was a sort of freedom: I did not have to ask anyone if I could wear this or that. And there was some sort of authority as well: I had control of the household, servants and so on. In my rather limited and innocent vision at the time, I did not realize that there was a world beyond mine too, and that it was full of violence.

My mother sang a lot and one of her favourite songs, a Punjabi marriage song, which imparts a piece of advice from a mother to her daughter, often comes back to me. The mother says, 'Dear child, your days of joy are now over and you are leaving the warmth of your parents' home. You are going to a strange place where no one will care for you, no one will listen to you. Tread carefully, my child, be respectful and create a place for yourself through humility and respect.' The pathos of that song often comes back to me when I look beyond my own life into the lives of those innumerable women who are tortured for dowry, who are at the mercy of callous relatives and have nowhere to go. Their only relief is death.

Nowhere in marriage is the woman considered to be a human being with feelings, needs and desires. I remember once being shocked because the young son of a neighbour of ours said he was getting married because his mother was very ill and they needed someone in the house to do the housework. I wondered then if this was all the young woman meant to him, a home help. I asked the young man sarcastically why his mother had not married rather than him. Predictably, he wasn't amused.

As I walked home from his wedding ceremony, I

remembered another incident that had made me really angry. I was waiting at a bus stop when I heard some women talking about a young man who was looking for a bride. 'Three girls have been offered to my son. I am tempted to accept the one from Mussoorie.' 'Yes, yes, auntie,' replied the other women, 'let's take the one from Mussoorie, at least we'll have some place to go to in the summer.'

At the time I was not involved in the anti-dowry agitation, yet the word 'offer' had irritated me. I remember thinking, she's talking as if someone is offering her fried fish on a plate. Little did I know then how true this was, for that, sadly, is the attitude: here's a piece of fish or whatever; if you don't like it, throw it away, you can always get a replacement.'

In recent years, the anti-dowry agitation seems to have gone into a sort of decline. Yet, the number of cases of dowry-related violence and dowry deaths continues to rise. Earlier, we had believed—and perhaps we were wrong in doing so—that dowry was largely a middle-class problem and it related only to Hindu families, mostly from North India. Today, we have been disabused of this notion as dowry continues to spread its tentacles far and wide and we hear stories of Muslim, Christian and Sikh women who are suffering because of dowry. Meanwhile, the courts continue to be prejudiced and unfair, and convictions are so rare as to be almost negligible. And within the women's movement too, there are now differences of opinion, with prominent women claiming that dowry is something that is actually pro-women, rather than against them. When I listen to such statements I don't know whether to be resigned that we have, once again, come full circle, or despair that we have made such little progress, or hopeful that these differences are at least beginning to lead to a debate, which hopefully will make us wiser and more capable of addressing such issues. I leave you with this question.